New
Adult a

90 0872518 6

Jovita M. Ross-Gordon
COEDITORS-IN-CHIEF

Negotiating Eth
Practice in Adul
Education

Elizabeth J. Burge

EDITOR

Number 123 • Fall 2009
Jossey-Bass
San Francisco

NEGOTIATING ETHICAL PRACTICE IN ADULT EDUCATION
Elizabeth J. Burge (ed.)
New Directions for Adult and Continuing Education, no. 123
Susan Imel, Jovita M. Ross-Gordon, Coeditors-in-Chief

Microfilm copies of issues and articles are available in 16mm and 35mm, as well as microfiche in 105mm, through University Microfilms Inc., 300 North Zeeb Road, Ann Arbor, Michigan 48106-1346.

NEW DIRECTIONS FOR ADULT AND CONTINUING EDUCATION (ISSN 1052-2891, electronic ISSN 1536-0717) is part of The Jossey-Bass Higher and Adult Education Series and is published quarterly by Wiley Subscription Services, Inc., A Wiley Company, at Jossey-Bass, 989 Market Street, San Francisco, California 94103-1741. Periodicals Postage Paid at San Francisco, California, and at additional mailing offices. POSTMASTER: Send address changes to New Directions for Adult and Continuing Education, Jossey-Bass, 989 Market Street, San Francisco, California 94103-1741.

New Directions for Adult and Continuing Education is indexed in CIJE: Current Index to Journals in Education (ERIC); Contents Pages in Education (T&F); ERIC Database (Education Resources Information Center; Higher Education Abstracts (Claremont Graduate University); and Sociological Abstracts (CSA/CIG).

SUBSCRIPTIONS cost $98.00 for individuals and $269.00 for institutions, agencies, and libraries.

EDITORIAL CORRESPONDENCE should be sent to the Coeditors-in-Chief, Susan Imel, ERIC/ACVE, 1900 Kenny Road, Columbus, Ohio 43210-1090, e-mail: imel.l@osu.edu; or Jovita M. Ross-Gordon, Southwest Texas State University, EAPS Dept., 601 University Drive, San Marcos, TX 78666.

Cover photograph by Jack Hollingsworth@Photodisc

www.josseybass.com

CONTENTS

EDITOR'S NOTES

In 1988 the first book about applied ethics in adult education contexts appeared (Brockett). Sixteen years later, Brockett and Hiemstra (2004) issued their own decision-making model. Now, just five years on, you hold the reflections of other experienced and well-known authors, but this time including an internationally known philosopher, Anthony Weston. In between these book formats, also on the road to more thinking about applied ethics in adult education, lie many articles, chapters, and other publications, for which Thomas J. Sork's chapter is your travel guide.

Before you jump into the goodies ahead, stay a moment with me. Why another book, now? It is time, I believe, to produce a new condensed review of the literature (Sork), gather frank narratives and personal reflections from more leaders in our field (Sue Folinsbee, Talmadge C. Guy, Catherine A. Hansman, and Tom Heaney), and gain a meta-reflection from another highly regarded adult educator (Arthur L. Wilson). It is definitely time now to broaden the vision even more and invite a professional philosopher into our field. Finally, it is time to enlarge our place in the growing field of applied ethics generally.

Applied ethics is discussed in generalized approaches (Johnson and Ridley, 2008; La Follette, 2005; Quinn, 2005; Singer, 1999), and in terms of the professions ("professional ethics") for managing regulation of activity, quality, credentialing, and matters of client-professional trust (Luban, 2003; Martin, 2000). Additional book format material, useful for scanning for links to our field, has emerged in specific fields of practice such as medicine (Somerville, 2006), technology use (Cavalier, 2005; Tavani, 2006), education (Beckner, 2004; Nash, 1996), the environment (Light and Rolston, 2002; Weston, 2009), multicultural contexts (Cooper, 2004), and workplaces (Rowson, 2006). Almond's definition of applied ethics usually sets my students off into long discussion:

> Ethical decision-making seen as practical policy that consciously recognizes the constraints of moral norms, rights, and ethical principles capable of commanding universal respect . . . the object of applied ethics is . . . to gain clearer perceptions of right and wrong, with a view to embodying these insights in manners and institutions [2005, pp. 26–27].

But not everyone would agree, given some authors' predilections toward framing ethical issues as dilemmas of opposing rights (Beckner, 2004; Kidder, 1995) or others who refuse such blatant dichotomies and

WILEY
InterScience®
DISCOVER SOMETHING GREAT

NEW DIRECTIONS FOR ADULT AND CONTINUING EDUCATION, no. 123, Fall 2009 © 2009 Wiley Periodicals, Inc.
Published online in Wiley InterScience (www.interscience.wiley.com) • DOI: 10.1002/ace.338

1

insist on taking broader and deeper analyses with more creative intent (Weston chapter).

Despite today's applied ethics literature and earlier adult education efforts to render ethical thinking more practical and accessible (e.g., Brockett & Hiemstra, 2004; Brockett, 1988), my adult education graduate students hunger for more delicious workplace "trench" stories and for narratives that show their colleagues 'fessing up to ethical difficulties and tweaks of conscience, not to mention taking courageous or even dangerous stands. They arrive in classes from mostly instrumentalist or profit-driven approaches to learning over which they have little or no control. They need to be prompted to get past descriptions of what happened and get into self- and action-based reflection before any serious problematizing into ethical issues is possible. We engage in spirited and heated discussions about everyday ethics, even though none of us have formal training in philosophy. We discuss various ethical theories and values, such as Weston's "family of moral values" (2001, pp. 68–82) or Pratt's "types of commitment . . . justice, caring, and duty" (1998, pp. 116, 117). The spirit nests in their naming and claiming some hidden but driving values of their practice. The "heat" (both cognitive and affective) arrives during what feels like archaeological thinking prompted by my "brain-burning questions" (as one student put it): peeling away the many layers of factors and dynamics in ethically problematic situations and arguing about the merit of published codes of practice. They dig deeply enough to understand Pratt's point that many ethical issues lie in wait for unwary teachers—for example, in how "we choose to represent our content . . . the kind of relationships we form with learners . . . [and] whenever we challenge someone's world view" (p. 115).

But such digging is hard work sometimes. I too feel the heat from students unused to being asked to pick up their cognitive spades and dig up questions about course content (Caffarella, 1988). Nash's argument for a comprehensive analysis of contextual influences on ethical situations and subsequent decision making becomes better understood: "Every resolution to an ethical dilemma, I maintain, must consider the act, the intention, the circumstance, the principles, the beliefs, the outcomes, the virtues, the narrative, the community, and the political structures" (1996, p. 20). Anthony Weston's chapter definitely will help our thinking along such lines.

Two more disclosures are needed, apart from my concerns with some students being unable or unwilling to move into critical reflection. First, it seems to me that ethical issues in our field are not diminishing but expanding as increasing pressures for survival, competitive edges, and profit-maintenance squeeze institutions and companies and push the trend for outsourced teaching. The seductive effects of new technology persuade administrators to use monotechnology thinking for economical forms of course delivery (Burge, 2001). But is our intellectual energy and institutional support strong enough for us to dig into the sources of potential ethical hazards, benign as matters may appear on the surface? Some students tell me that they are tired of monotechnology thinking—that is, all their courses being online—but they know that it is a revenue generator (read, cheaper) option for their institutions. So who really benefits, ultimately, and who feels less advantaged? Where are the trade-offs needed to accommodate, ethically, the interests of all the parties concerned? The second disclosure links to the self- and group-regulatory duties of many professional organizations. Like many of my students and some of my colleagues, I remain unconvinced about codes of conduct for what is not officially a self-regulated occupation. Because you will read about codes in Thomas J. Sork's chapter, here is an advance opinion about codes that for me, at least, prompts further thought.

There are several reasons codes and rules for doing the right thing as a professional are disappointing in real-life practice: (1) ethical quandaries are complex and their resolution often nuanced and resistant to simple rules; (2) ethical quandaries are fluid and demand considerable flexibility on the part of the professional; (3) professionals often encounter competing obligations to individuals, organizations, and society at large, and there often are good reasons for different courses of action; (4) being ethical is a continuous process, not merely a right answer; and (5) ethical decisions are made by fallible human beings, many of whom are motivated by self-interest, defensiveness, and a remarkable capacity to justify unethical courses of action" (Johnson and Ridley, 2008, p. xvii).

All the more reason for me, as just one adult educator, to work more on my own ability to interrogate a context for its layers of ethical problems and figure out possible, creative responses. And to help my students do the same. You will decide for yourself, of course, but the need to be a self-aware, critical, and independent ethical thinker is one of the threads of this volume.

Time to jump in. The volume is designed as a cumulating sequence, but you may prefer to dip into chapters and build from there. If you want to gain a quick footing in applied ethics without being scared away, then it is Anthony Weston's engaging chapter you need. A self-described "professional ethical philosopher," he asks us to think at a meta-level—about how we think about our ethical thinking. He argues persuasively for less use of the judgmental and limiting mind-set of analysis-by-dilemma, for more critical reviewing of known ethical theories such as utilitarianism or rights or caring, and for a creative engagement with new possibilities: "If we care so deeply about both utilities and rights, oughtn't we spend our intellectual and practical energy to redesign our institutions so that these two types of values conflict less often and less viciously?" (p. 14). He carries his own meta-reflection into his reflections in the four narrative chapters.

Thomas J. Sork's chapter also asks us to step back, but chronologically this time into his view of a quarter-century of adult education literature about applied ethics. Arguing that "adult education has developed more as a field of practice than a profession and there is continuing debate about whether any further 'professionalization' of the field is desirable," he reviews the attempts to design and implement codes of conduct, first de novo and then associated with efforts to find out what practitioners actually identified as ethical concerns. You have enough detail here to compare these published values with your own values. Review the often "morally hazardous terrain" of adult education through the models for decision making that attract Sork's attention.

Alternatively, if you look for deliciously detailed reflections from the trenches of practice, go to the four narrative chapters by Sue Folinsbee, Talmadge C. Guy, Catherine A. Hansman, and Tom Heaney. Appreciate the courageous honesty in their stories. Learn of the values and contextual assessments that helped drive their assessments of possible options. Folinsbee uses five ethical principles to guide her actions. But as a very experienced workplace practitioner, she knows that "although principles remain steadfast, the practice we engage in needs to be flexible." So follow her through three sets of rigorous self-reflections about her ethical behavior. Walk with Talmadge C. Guy to see how "systems of unmerited privilege constantly nip at the edges of my practice." Hear his vivid examples of student attitudes and behaviors that impose serious issues in how he must "value, evaluate, and balance different points of view." See why he is concerned about an "unfettered ethical commitment to democratic educational practice," despite that principle seeming so worthy and innocent. Catherine A. Hansman's unflinching appraisals of her experiences with mentoring situations are also riveting reading. "How does an adult educator unpack ethical issues within mentoring contexts, especially when those issues nest in interpersonal relationships?" As with all these writers, her courage lies in facing up to many ethical issues that nest in complex analyses of all relevant contextual factors, not the least of which are some deep-seated human needs for safety and growth. Tom Heaney's grassroots social justice experience has helped him excavate some covert dynamics of many ethical problems. He asks a question that resonates with the analyses from the other three: "As educators, we are seldom free agents. We are employed by and expected to represent the interests of educational institutions that are components of a larger social infrastructure and that are, in complex and frequently hidden ways, dominated by corporate and political interests." Consider Heaney's definition of "good work" in adult education practice, and see how far you agree with his single guiding question. Confronted with having to choose between difficult choices of action, he asked himself, "How do I weigh these consequences? Or do I succumb to paralysis in the face of difficult choices?"

Arthur L. Wilson reflects thoughtfully on the preceding four chapters and the Weston chapter. His own reflection on why he left after eleven years of teaching in an adult learning center carries a particular disappointment related to social and political structures: "A chief one was this deep-seated sense of philosophical and ethical malaise that, despite what I thought were the right values, hopes, and efforts, I came to believe I was, fundamentally, doing a bad job." Wilson sees strong links in the chapters to three themes of reflection, power, and negotiation, but he argues that adult educators need to do more work in searching out societal structural dissonances and conflicts: "to make radical shifts in how we understand our roles in the production and reproduction of systems which, in practice, may work against our expressed intentions. Thus we develop ethical issues because of a lack of congruence or integrity."

Finally, read the synthesis for lessons and reflections to carry you into more expeditions of the archaeology of your ethics. Feel inspired.

References

Almond, B. "Applied ethics." In E. Craig (ed.), *The Shorter Routledge Encyclopaedia of Philosophy*. London, Routledge, 2005.

Beckner, W. *Ethics for Educational Leaders*. Boston: Allyn & Bacon, 2004.

Brockett, R. G. (ed.). *Ethical Issues in Adult Education*. New York: Teachers College Press, 1988.

Brockett, R. G., and Hiemstra, R. *Toward Ethical Practice*. Malabar, Fla.: Krieger, 2004.

Burge, E. J. "Using Learning Technologies: A Synthesis of Challenges and Guidelines." In E. J. Burge and M. Haughey (eds.), *Using Learning Technologies: International Perspectives on Practice*. London: RoutledgeFalmer, 2001.

Caffarella, R. S. "Ethical Dilemmas in the Teaching of Adults." In R. G. Brockett (ed.), *Ethical Issues in Adult Education*. New York: Teachers College Press, 1988.

Cavalier, R. J. (ed.). *The Impact of the Internet on Our Moral Lives*. Buffalo: State University of New York Press, 2005.

Cooper, D. E. *Ethics for Professionals in a Multicultural World*. Upper Saddle River, NJ: Pearson/Prentice Hall, 2004.

Johnson, W. B., and Ridley, C. R. *The Elements of Ethics*. New York: Palgrave Macmillan, 2008.

Kidder, R. *How Good People Make Tough Choices: Resolving the Dilemmas of Ethical Living*. New York: Fireside, 1995.

La Follette, H. *The Oxford Handbook of Practical Ethics*. New York: Oxford University Press, 2005.

Light, A, and Rolston, H. (eds.). *Environmental Ethics: An Anthology*. San Francisco/Oxford: Wiley-Blackwell, 2002.

Luban, D. "Professional ethics." In R. G. Frey and C. H. Wellman (eds.), *A Companion to Applied Ethics*. Oxford, UK: Blackwell, 2003.

Martin, M. W. *Meaningful Work: Rethinking Professional Ethics*. Oxford, UK: Oxford University Press, 2000.

Nash, R. J. *"Real World" Ethics: Frameworks for Educators and Human Service Professionals*. New York: Teachers College Press, 1996.

Pratt, D. D. "Ethical Reasoning in Teaching Adults." In M. W. Galbraith (ed.), *Adult Learning Methods: A Guide for Effective Instruction*. Malabar, Fla.: Krieger, 1998.

Quinn, M. J. *Ethics for the Information Age* (2nd ed). Boston: Addison Wesley, 2005.

Rowson, R. *Working Ethics: How to Be Fair in a Culturally Complex World*. London: Jessica Kingsley, 2006.

Singer, P. *Practical Ethics* (2nd ed). Cambridge, UK: Cambridge University Press, 1999.

Somerville, M. *The Ethical Imagination: CBC Massey Lectures*. Toronto: House of Anansi/Groundwood, 2006.

Tavani, H. T. *Ethics and Technology: Ethical Issues in an Age of Information and Communication Technology* (2nd ed). San Francisco: Wiley, 2006.

Weston, A. *A 21st Century Ethical Toolbox.* New York: Oxford University Press, 2001. (2nd ed., 2007, now available)

Weston, A. *The Incompleat Eco-philosopher: Essays from the Edges of Environmental Ethics.* Albany: State University of New York Press, 2009.

ELIZABETH J. BURGE is a professor in adult education at the University of New Brunswick in Atlantic Canada and a community social activist.

1

Ethical issues in adult education are often open-ended, complex, problematic situations. The real question is not which side is right, or to which moral choice principle we must appeal, but simply how we can engage those situations intelligently and constructively.

For a Meta-Ethics as Good as Our Practice

Anthony Weston

Consider two scenarios of ethical problems in adult education.

> An adult education consultant is asked to run a five-day workshop in an expensive resort, with his business class airfares prepaid. The company requesting the event is a major international enterprise, well regarded in the corporate world, but the consultant disagrees strongly with the company's policies about labor hiring in developing countries. Frankly, however, his client list would be enhanced if he accepted the company's invitation.

> A planned community educational project involves spending a lot of money on the use of various new technologies, but you know that the intended client group will have difficulties in getting regular access to such equipment once the project has begun. You also believe that after the initial funding has run out, there will be no money for continuous maintenance and updating of the technology. You think about walking away from this project on ethical grounds.

Liz Burge kindly offered these cases, among others, in response to my query about representative ethical puzzles in the field. I found them enlightening indeed, but also, from a resolutely practical point of view anyway, perhaps not quite so puzzling. In both cases my view is that going ahead—accepting the invitation, staying with the project—is much wiser than walking away. True, there are concerns about keeping one's own hands clean, so to speak. But it is also true that walking away does almost nothing

NEW DIRECTIONS FOR ADULT AND CONTINUING EDUCATION, no. 123, Fall 2009 © 2009 Wiley Periodicals, Inc.
Published online in Wiley InterScience (www.interscience.wiley.com) • DOI: 10.1002/ace.339

else. In the first case, the company's labor practices will be unaffected; in the second case, the new technologies are apparently being implemented anyway. To actually make any kind of difference, the adult educator needs to stay involved. *Go* to the workshop, in the first case, but go precisely as an advocate for changing the company's labor practices. Who knows that this is not what the inviters (some of them, anyway) might even be hoping for? And *stay* with the new technology project, in the second case, making the argument for better access from the inside. We are spending all this money, but have we overlooked getting, and keeping, the people connected to the technology? Well, there's the obvious next step . . . and who better to carry that brief than you?

Granted, these answers might change if we knew more particulars. Sometimes visibly declining such an invitation can also create useful pressure to make change, or highlight potential ethical problems that staying involved would not. I am not saying that we ought to stick with any process under any conditions. Still, on the face of it so far, these cases seem to call for ethical *engagement*: for an ongoing process of advocacy and involvement, rather than pulling out in the name of (one understanding of) ethics. For our consideration now, they might also prompt us to further explore our understanding of the general goals and character of ethics itself.

The Imperative to Judge

By "meta-ethics" philosophers mean a set of views about what ethics is, how it may be grounded, and why we need it (Sayre-McCord, 2007). Thus an *ethics* may deliver certain moral judgments (such as: adult educators should not walk away from tainted deals just to keep their hands clean), while a *meta-ethics* offers a vision of the goals and character of ethics itself (as in: the task of ethics is to make a constructive difference in the world) such that those judgments in turn get a context and at least the beginnings of a justification.

Meta-ethical views may not be framed explicitly at all. Normally they function more as background assumptions when we think about ethics. Fair enough: thinking about ethics is hard enough without having to think about thinking about ethics too. Homesteading this particular conceptual countryside can usually be safely left to philosophers. But there are times when meta-ethical reconsideration can be critical. Certain meta-ethical assumptions may unduly confine or even contort our ethical thinking and practice. They may need to be challenged and changed. And so it may be here.

One seemingly obvious and even rock-bottom meta-ethical assumption is this: that ethics' main task is to *judge* certain kinds of situations. A widespread and usually taken-for-granted view is that ethics is something like a system of verdicts. From early on we learn to take questions like "Is X right or wrong?" as the paradigmatic ethical questions, where X is usually something we think we already know all about: gay marriage, maybe, or eating animals or capital punishment or driving a carbon-belching SUV as the planet warms. Morally speaking, we seem to be happy enough to pass judgment on such questions without a lot of detail or exploration—but we *do* seem to suppose that they definitely and urgently need our opinion. College students, for instance, regularly come into my ethics classes expecting a lot of debate about moral issues and cases, either with the aim of settling their own ethical views about contentious matters or of setting their classmates straight on the Moral Truth. Give them even a one-sentence description of a moral problem and they already are chafing at the bit to decide about it and to argue. This doesn't strike them as odd or precipitous at all. When the class turns out to be heading in an entirely different direction (we almost never strictly *argue* at all, but instead seek ways to act effectively and intelligently in the face of complexity and contention, and specifically welcome a diversity of views as a truer reflection of the nature of our values and as a way of enriching and strengthening collective action) it takes some serious readjustment.

To be able to definitively judge a situation, moreover, we must also think of it as essentially fixed, "given," rather than itself in flow and open to change through ongoing engagement. To respectably pass judgment we have to suppose that the situation is not going to evolve into something quite different while we're doing so, or be affected by the judgment itself. It's as if the situation stands apart from us, like a finished work of art or a supposedly well-defined historical deed, nothing we can now affect, so that, once again, the only kind of response it really invites is passing judgment. This is another reason, perhaps, why we are so remarkably incurious about further details: as with art works, the situation or scenario, however simple, aspires to self-sufficiency. More details might just confuse the main moral points or unbalance the presentation. It's ours only to stand back and evaluate.

Consider again, then, the two adult education scenarios with which we began. Being so very simplified and "fixed," they too do not welcome further questioning (such as: Where and how in each case might you be able to make change by working from the inside?) and, set up as they are for classroom use, they too invite the only kind of response that the usual classroom allows: passing judgment, followed by arguments pro or con. Moreover, the scenarios themselves must be held as "given" in order to do so. We are emphatically *not* invited to explore or experiment with them (in the first case, for example, is the corporation really so morally monolithic? and so on) or even to look at the opportunity costs of acting on different judgments (that is, to explore what possibilities are foreclosed by specific choices, such as walking away).

All of this sets in so quickly and readily that we scarcely even notice we have immediately fallen right into one particular way of taking up such problems. Yet other quite different kinds of responses are possible. Other professionals—auto mechanics, say, or marriage counselors or business strategists—would never for a moment think that their main job is simply to pass summative judgment on simplified scenarios, let alone that an acceptable reason for action (or, more likely, inaction) might be to just keep their own hands clean. No: on their views, problems are precisely cases in which something is not working out (a car, a marriage, some marketing campaign) and the professionals' job is to figure out how to *help*, complex and uncertain and somewhat compromised as that help will probably prove to be. Those complexities and compromises become not reasons to overly puzzle over the proper judgment, or to pull out if some preexisting standards are not met, but instead good reasons to soft-pedal such judgmentalism in the first place and stay attentively and resolutely involved. Why couldn't ethics be like *that*?

Dilemma-ism

The usual meta-ethical undertow becomes still stronger when we turn to the most classic ethical situations and scenarios: ethical *dilemmas*.

> A woman was near death from cancer. One drug might save her, a form of radium that a druggist in the same town had discovered. The druggist was charging $2,000, ten times what the drug cost him to make. The sick woman's husband, Heinz, went to everyone he knew to borrow the money, but he could only get together about half of what it cost. He told the druggist that his wife was dying and asked him to sell it cheaper or let him pay later. But the druggist said "no." The husband got desperate and broke into the man's store to steal the drug for his wife. Should the husband have done that? Why? [Kohlberg, 1969, p. 379].

This is the psychologist Lawrence Kohlberg's famous "Heinz Dilemma," designed, along with other similar moral dilemmas, to probe the development of our moral thinking. Kohlberg insists on using such dilemmas and *only* such dilemmas to probe moral thinking *as such*. Thus he seems to suppose that the paradigmatic moral problem involves two and only two sides, deeply and inevitably opposed to each other, each unsatisfactorily narrow but irreconcilable, so that we are left choosing the lesser of two evils, the less incomplete of two partial alternatives, the least tragic tragedy. The meta-ethical assumptions so far discussed have clearly kicked in here: dilemmas are emphatically "fixed" situations, and the whole tragedy is that we supposedly must just choose—judge—one way or the other. But Kohlberg's insistence on framing moral cases in terms of dilemmas represents a further and radical simplification as well. The dilemma structure reduces the contending sides or values down to *two* and correspondingly exacerbates their opposition. Everything is painted in the starkest terms.

This reduction is not limited to Kohlberg. Today you can hardly even mention the word "moral" to anyone without "dilemma" coming up in the next sentence, if it waits that long. At least one leading textbook in practical

New Directions for Adult and Continuing Education • DOI: 10.1002/ace

ethics literally *requires* the framing of issues in terms of dilemmas (Rothman, 2005), as if there is no other form in which a moral issue might *ever* show up or be better understood. In just the same way, when Kohlberg and his co-researchers encountered subjects (disproportionately girls, it turned out) who asked for more details about the alleged dilemma rather than just delivering their verdict, or suggested options for Heinz other than stealing the drug *or* just letting his wife die, the researchers actually classified them as morally immature; that is, the researchers concluded they literally didn't understand ethics itself (Gilligan, 1993).

Yet it is possible, all the same, that those girls understood the alleged dilemma quite well—arguably even better than the researchers, supposedly empiricists, who apparently did not for a moment question their own understanding of ethics even when confronted with such richly suggestive and after all quite empirical data. The situation really does have many unexplored aspects and options, and it invites many modes of engagement besides just two. Maybe Heinz could barter his skills or time in place of the money he can't raise. Or maybe he could call up a newspaper and embarrass the druggist, or raise the money through public appeal. Moreover, is Heinz really the only one who can act in this situation? Does he (or whoever) really act in a social vacuum? What about charitable or governmental assistance? Do he and his wife have a religious congregation or workplace community that could help? Have they no insurance? If not, why not? What can *we* do to not only to help Heinz's wife but also to make medical care more readily available to all in such dire straits?

A group of health care professionals in one of my workshops once pointed out that because most state laws require prisons to offer medical treatment to inmates, Heinz's wife could steal the drug herself and try to get arrested for it, so that one way or the other she gets what she needs. On the other hand, it is not clear that she should really want the drug in the first place; apparently it has not been tested. Where's the FDA when you need it? Maybe she should get it free as a demonstration, a test case. Meanwhile, has Heinz found out why the druggist is holding out (maybe he needs the money for further drug development)? Speaking of talking to people, it's also not clear that Heinz has even asked his own wife what she wants. Maybe she's suffering enough that she's ready to go, and Heinz's moral hyperactivity is only a symptom of his own denial.

Of course we can redescribe such situations to (try to) preclude any other alternatives or complexities from coming up. Philosophers like such dilemmas for pedagogical purposes—the stark choices they present cast ethical theories into a clear light—and so it is easy to get invested in starkness for its own sake. True enough: if you start with the *assumption* that Heinz's situation is a dilemma, then you can certainly doctor it to keep it so, if only by devising some ad hoc way of ruling out whatever other alternatives are suggested, or ruling out the people who suggest them. But this is question begging from the point of view of ethics in general. The question is whether our ethical values *are* really so sharply opposed in the first place. The pragmatic philosopher John Dewey argued that ethical problems are more like large, vague regions of tension, not at all distinct or well defined (Dewey, 1939; Gouinlock, 1976). No closure can really be expected. But ethical problems are also, for just the same reason, regions of opportunity. Constructively engaging the problem, trying to change it into something more manageable, making something of the opportunities, is the most intelligent response—often the *only* intelligent or "mature" response (Weston, 2007, 2008). We can and must take some actual responsibility for making the world a better place—not just judge someone else's (say, Heinz's) response to the world as it is, and then think that somehow ethics' job is done.

A Meta-Ethical Reorientation

I am sure that a few situations really are dilemmas. In general, though, I want to suggest that we live in a much more open world: a world in which ethical problems, like most of life's challenges, invite us into a broader field of possibility. Constructive ethical thinking and action should try, in general, to maximize and make the best use of this openness—not to regret or close it down.

Reaching moral verdicts is *one* task of ethics. Articulate, well-considered and passionate judgments are sometimes just what a situation demands, and there is a place for practicing this form of judgment in the classroom as well. The problem, though, is that too often we allow judgment to fill the screen, as if ethics were about nothing else. In fact, even when judgment *is* the main imperative, it will be a very dodgy kind of judgment indeed if it insists on delivering verdicts on barely sketched situations without experimenting with and exploring them, leaving room also for uncertainty and new developments.

Exploration, in short, is also a key task of ethics—in addition to and sometimes instead of judgment. Another little story may help here. A student just back from Bolivia told me one day last year that the practice among young Bolivian males is to go to a prostitute for their sexual initiation. He was disturbed by this and wanted my opinion—my judgment. In fact I am pretty sure he wanted me to confirm and second his own outrage. Outrage is appropriate, no doubt, especially from the point of view of a society still struggling to value women as full partners and equals. Once again, though, the problem is that the insistence on making such judgments pretty much closes down the discussion. Nothing else is explored; we think we've said everything that needs to be said. So, playing teacher, I said, well, let's see what might be *learned*, even and maybe especially from situations like this.

We kept talking. It turned out that when my student expressed his surprise and confusion to his Bolivian friends, they challenged him to explain and defend sexual initiation in America. He didn't really know how to answer. This, we eventually decided, was the real source of much of his confusion—and a much more useful question. We don't have much say over Bolivian men, after all, but we *can* make a difference to what we ourselves do. Do we really think that sexual initiation works very well in our own country? How do *we* teach young people about sex, anyway? Locker-room conversation? Movies? Pornography? How realistic or helpful or ethical are these? What would be better? Questions like these never even come up if we think that our job is just to judge other people's practices, as if from some safe and unaffected Archimedean point, and then, well, stop.

Engagement with others, in ongoing moral discussion, is another key task of ethics. We say we believe in dialogue, but we do very poorly in actually talking to each other when serious disagreements are involved. The only real models in the culture are talk-show scream-fests and political demonstrations, where the aim is not to work through differences or use them constructively but rather to exhibit or even exacerbate them. Among other things, what is revealed here is a disinterest in ethical engagement as a *process*. Some issue is at stake, of course, but it is also true that dialogue itself, ongoing, respectful, and open-ended, has ethical value and needs skillful tending. This is how we build and rebuild civic relationships and social and political community, as well as our individual relationships and our small-scale communities, in families or with co-workers, and in the adult education classroom. Here too, in another way, it should be clear that the task of ethical discussion is not merely or even mainly to "resolve" some particular issue but in general to sustain the moral community itself. Notice too: *this* goal might well require deliberately leaving some issues *unresolved*.

When issues come up not as dilemmas but genuinely understood as open-ended, complex, problematic situations, the question of which side is "right" is unbearably crude and may even become a way of *not* engaging the problem itself. A simple verdict becomes a substitute for actually getting involved. A better question is whether there are ways in which many of the values in play might be compatible, might combine, play off each other, synergize. Thus, as I put it, a key task of ethics is also to help *integrate values* (Weston, 2008).

Suppose that instead of trying to figure out which side is right, we begin to ask what *each* side is right *about*. Then we may be able to find some common ground, or at least some creative ways to shift the problem toward matters that we can do something about—together. Even the toughest and most contentious issues look utterly different when they can be seen not as competitions to claim the mantle of moral truth but as explorations of the complexity of truth, each side speaking for something important, not necessarily incompatible—as for example, to immediately take the hardest case, in the abortion debate, where no one on either side really denies the preciousness of *both* life *and* choice (Weston, 2008). Viewed from the point of view of both-and rather than either-or, the debate looks entirely different. Passionate defenders of life, after all, would hardly rest content if *Roe* v. *Wade* were merely overturned. There are a host of other things to do: strengthen the family, enhance prenatal and postnatal care, speak to the hypersexualization of everything teenaged. Likewise, passionate defenders of abortion rights would hardly rest content if *Roe* were secured. Once again there are a host of other things to do, such as, um, strengthening the family, enabling adequate prenatal and postnatal care, and speaking to the hypersexualization of everything teenaged, as well as equal access to child care, family leave policies, and rethinking the relations between the sexes in general. Disagreements remain, of course, even fundamental ones, but the "big pictures" are not pure and simple opposites. There is room for shared agendas here as well. Real moral values complexify, overlap, draw us back into connection and interdependence, and thus make it possible to go forward *together.*

Ethical Theories

Adult educators with some exposure to traditional philosophical ethics will probably remember, above all, some *theories* of ethics: basic principles that claim to unify our moral values and give us clear direction about a basis on which to make ethical decisions. Utilitarianism, for example: an emphasis on happiness, quantified where possible, extended into the basic principle of the greatest good of the greatest number. Classically opposed to utilitarian thinking is deontology or rights theory, insisting that no one is to be treated as a mere means to others' ends, but instead that persons (and possibly other beings) have a dignity that demands respect—hence, rights (Weston, 2008).

How do such theories fit into the context of the meta-ethical reorientation I am suggesting here? In one way, they don't. Ethical theories typically think of themselves as complete, self-sufficient, and therefore mutually exclusive. Reading the modest and nuanced ethical tensions of our everyday problems through theoretical eyes therefore seriously risks escalating those tensions into sweeping philosophical stand-offs. The Heinz Dilemma, for example, as I've noted, is usually supposed to illustrate the clash of utilitarianism (Heinz's wife's life) versus rights (the druggist's property rights). I have suggested, however, that it is not at all necessary—and in fact is unfortunate and disabling—to read Heinz's situation in such oppositional terms. Likewise we also may need to resist and rethink the implicit dilemma-ism of this use of ethical theories generally. From the point of view of constructive engagement, even a straight-out conflict of theories is not somehow necessarily a mandate for *judgment.* "Social reconstruction," to use Dewey's apt phrase, is often a much better response. If we care so deeply about both utilities and rights, oughtn't we expend our intellectual and practical energy to redesign our institutions so that these two types of values conflict less often and less viciously? This is arguably one of the aims of modern systems of public provision, for example. Oughtn't ethics therefore be reimagining the design of (say) the health care payment system (for example)? Or again, if air and water were cleaner, fewer cancers and therefore fewer dilemmas such as the Heinz case would arise in the first place. Environmental ethics would be served as well. Again, it's not that dilemmas would necessarily go away, but there are certainly other and more productive tasks for our moral energies and resources in the face of them.

In my view, then, ethical theories are not to be used to underwrite or mandate particular judgments, let alone as argumentative bludgeons against other theories. But they do have their uses. The most important of these is to help us *articulate* certain especially important values. Certain of our values do hang together in tight and sometimes even logical ways. General philosophical articulations of those subsets of values, and some attempt at consistency within those subsets, can therefore help us organize our values and also rethink and perhaps shift certain outliers. Still, no such theoretical organization precludes other theories or other values less readily or less naturally theorized. There is no reason that values in general must even be consistent; it may just be that we simply value a variety of sometimes-conflicting things. It would better to actually *expect* ethical theories to give voice to some of these conflicts, rather than expecting ethical philosophy somehow to resolve them.

I would even suggest that part of the interest of ethical theories lies in this very particularity. They reflect not only the partiality of certain moral interests among others but also often specific times and places. For example, the supposedly timeless opposition between utilitarianism and deontology is also the opposition between a practical, humanistic, and liberal English temperament (John Stuart Mill) and a sterner and darker Germanic Protestantism (Immanuel Kant). But quite obviously—and luckily—there are other moral temperaments as well. Indeed, further ethical theories are also regularly being proposed, in fact, and move in and out of the theoretical canon. In the last fifty years or so, for instance, *virtue theories* are often added: theories concerned with character traits (self-discipline, responsibility, honesty, charity, loyalty; professional ethics; and so on). Their roots are ancient: Greek in particular, in the Western tradition, and Confucian in the Eastern. Still newer ethical theories highlight *relationships,* both particular relationships such as those within families or specific communities, as well as the human relationship to more-than-human nature. Each has something timely to add—and enough said.

Ethics in the Practice of Adult Education

Well-grounded and subtle skills are at work in the essays by adult educators featured in this volume. Each practitioner is sensitive to a rich range of values and aware of underlying structural issues. They use inventive and transformative methods, patiently and persistently, to help their students find their own voices and realize their powers. They are sensitive to complexity, to multiple hidden possibilities, and to the inevitable open-endedness of all their actions in the world. Such practitioners are already, I believe, operating out of meta-ethical assumptions quite different from those I began with by identifying and criticizing, and closer to the alternatives I have been advancing in their place. Perhaps we might be one step more explicit about how and why.

Catherine Hansman attends carefully to the ethical complexities of the mentoring relationship. She makes it clear that much is at stake for both (all) parties, that multiple and overlapping relationships are in play, and above all that there is always more to be learned. Her approach reminds me of the feminist philosopher Margaret Walker's lovely characterization of ethics as "a collection of perceptive, imaginative, appreciative, and expressive skills and capacities which put us and keep us in contact with the realities of ourselves and specific others" (Walker, 1989, p. 21). Hansman also reminds us that all of these "skills and capacities" *develop*. It's not as though we are somehow "supposed to" have it all together from the beginning.

All of the authors here formulate "maxims" or "main principles" that they take to guide their practice. Sue Folinsbee's "principles," for example, are "ensuring worker and management commitment to a workplace education initiative, confidentiality, joint planning to get a clear understanding of the differing interests throughout the context, a holistic, asset-based approach, and voluntary participation" (Chapter Three in this volume). In my view, this is a laudable form of explicitness, without any need to classify these principles in turn under some broader theoretical heading. They are, after all, quite different from each other, they are all important, and they already stand at a workable level of abstraction. Words such as *principle* and *maxims* (Hansman) can sometimes tempt us to more abstraction—they may seem to invite a theoretical move—but again, on my view at least, being *articulate* about values is not at all the same thing as fitting them into an existing ethical theory or making them into a theory of their own. You're not somehow lacking if you can't trace your working values all the way back to some overarching ethical framework. You're just alert to the complexity of the real world.

Tom Heaney writes that:

> One ethical dilemma faced by educators committed to social justice can be how to maintain employment without compromising the values of equity and justice. . . . As educators . . . we are employed by and expected to represent the interests of educational institutions that are components of a larger social infrastructure and that are, in complex and frequently hidden ways, dominated by corporate and political interests. . . . My choice is guided by: whom will I serve? . . . The old labor organizing song, "Which Side Are You On?" crystallizes the ethical imperative. We are forced to take sides, but on what basis do we choose? [Chapter Six in this volume]

As a professional ethical philosopher, here is probably where I should be wrinkling up my brow and rolling out the big philosophical guns. What I actually think is that Heaney should give himself more credit. Things do not seem at all so stark or dichotomous when he describes his actual, in-context practice. He writes of trying to do an honest and democratic review of certain alternative schools (Gilchrist, Wentworth; you'll have to read his chapter) that happened to be unpopular with their system's chancellor but were, in Heaney's and their own eyes, doing a first-rate job. Right on; but it's not as though he didn't *also* serve the public good or the actual requirements of his job when he did so. We might better look at it the other way around: to do this kind of work is to attempt, at least, to be on *everyone's* "side"— even the chancellor's. Despite the problematic distribution of power in this case, Heaney finds a course that all parties, officially anyway, must recognize as ethical and appropriate: open, participatory inquiry.

Of course one can see such situations purely in terms of a sort of hydraulics of power, of assertion and counterassertion. I think there is some strategic advantage, though, as well as ethical clarity, in simply not playing that game (aware as we may nonetheless be of it). It's not so much a matter of choosing sides as of just doing the work before us as well as we can—as Heaney clearly does—and in the meantime resolutely and visibly expecting everyone else to approach it in the same way.

Back in the classroom, Talmadge Guy writes of the "ethical bind" between democratic participation in the classroom on the one hand and beginning to challenge unmerited and unrecognized privilege on the other. "I struggle," he says, "to navigate a course of action that is simultaneously inclusive of multiple views and multicultural and antiracist, antisexist" (Chapter Four of this volume).

For sure. But once again, I am not sure that is necessarily a "bind." *Both* "sides" matter; *both* are forms of respect for his (our) students and their work. To achieve them together is absolutely a pedagogical challenge, an opportunity, the very work itself. Of course it's difficult (Talmadge Guy: "Often, I find myself carefully calculating when and how to challenge majoritarian perspectives on race, class or gender. . . . I feel quite exhausted when I leave class and at times discouraged about my decision making"). I want to honor his commitment and self-awareness as a teacher, but also affirm that this is not somehow an ethical *problem,* exactly. It's not as though the values are unclear or that perhaps one or the other is really illegitimate or (as in Tom Heaney's case) has undue power behind it. Trying to honor both of these dimensions of the teacher's role just *is* ethical, already, all by itself.

Guy concludes:

> I try to strike a balance between my commitment to an ethic of racial justice and inclusion while using ethical strategies of inclusion, pluralism, and dialogue. I am also forced to strike a balance between my own positionality as

an African American male and my privilege, authority, and power as a male professor. There is no easy answer to either of these ethical challenges.

My suggestion is just a subtle difference of voice in that last sentence. Let us say: "There is no easy answer to either of these *pedagogical* challenges." The point is just this: *ethics* is not the problem. Guy, like the other adult educators represented here, is already doing profoundly and powerfully ethical work, and he knows exactly what is at stake: as usual, a "balance." He's already clearly working with that pedagogical challenge in experienced and able ways. This is the engagement of which I spoke in the beginning. This is all that ethics really does or can ask.

References

Dewey, J. *Theory of Valuation*. Chicago: University of Chicago Press, 1939.

Gilligan, C. *In a Different Voice*. Cambridge, Mass.: Harvard University Press, 1993.

Gouinlock. J. *The Moral Writings of John Dewey*. New York: Hafner Press, 1976.

Kohlberg, L. "Stage and Sequence: The Cognitive-Developmental Approach to Socialization." In D. A. Goslin (ed.), *Handbook of Socialization Theory and Research*. Chicago: Rand McNally, 1969.

Rothman, J. *From the Front Lines: Student Cases in Social Work Ethics*. Boston: Pearson/Allyn & Bacon, 2005.

Sayre-McCord, G. "Meta-Ethics." In *The Stanford Encyclopedia of Philosophy, 2007*. http://plato. stanford.edu/entries/metaethics/.

Walker, M. U. "Moral Understandings: Alternative 'Epistemology' for a Feminist Ethics." *Hypatia*, 1989, 4(2), 15–28.

Weston, A. *Creative Problem-Solving in Ethics*. Oxford/New York: Oxford University Press, 2007.

Weston, A. *A 21st Century Ethical Toolbox* (2nd ed.). Oxford/New York: Oxford University Press, 2008.

ANTHONY WESTON is professor of philosophy at Elon University in North Carolina, where he teaches ethics, Philosophy of education, environmental studies, and "millennial imagination."

2

This chapter surveys the growing body of literature on ethics and adult education, makes some critical observations about efforts to increase ethical sensitivity among practitioners, and offers guidance in how to deal with ethical dilemmas.

Applied Ethics in Adult and Continuing Education Literature

Thomas J. Sork

To someone who has been intrigued by the role of ethics in adult education for many years, it has been heartening to see how the field has responded to calls to address the ethical dimensions of practice. This response has taken many forms in the last twenty-five years, including explicit discussion of ethics in standard reference works (Lawson, 1996; Sork, 2005) and those dealing with philosophy and adult education (Elias and Merriam, 2005; Lawson, 1979), inclusion of ethics in specialized publications dealing with specific areas of practice such as administration (Galbraith, Sisco, and Guglielmino, 1997; Price, 1997; Sisco, 1988), program planning (Brockett and Hiemstra, 1998; Caffarella, 2002; Cervero and Wilson, 1994 and 2006; Singarella and Sork, 1983; Sork, 1988 and 2000; Wilson and Cervero, 1996), distance and online education (Burge, 2007; Holt, 1996 and 1998; Reed and Sork, 1990), marketing (Martel and Colley, 1986; Burns and Roche, 1988), continuing professional education (Felch, 1986; Lawler and Fielder, 1993; Lawler, 2000b, 2001; Pearson and Kennedy, 1985; Scanlan, 1985), teaching (Lenz, 1982; Pratt, 1998), human resource development and training (Maidment and Losito, 1980; Tarrant, 2001), evaluation (Brookfield, 1988), and in books and special issues of journals devoted to ethics (American Association of Adult and Continuing Education, AAACE, 1993; Brockett, 1988a; Brockett and Hiemstra, 2004; Jarvis, 1997). Although adult education may have been a little later than some in coming to terms with ethics, these developments occurred during a time when many other professions and occupations were struggling with the moral dimensions of

NEW DIRECTIONS FOR ADULT AND CONTINUING EDUCATION, no. 123, Fall 2009 © 2009 Wiley Periodicals, Inc.
Published online in Wiley InterScience (www.interscience.wiley.com) • DOI: 10.1002/ace.340

their practice and some philosophers were reaching out in very practical ways to their readers (Johnson and Ridley, 2008; Nash, 2002; Weston, 2005). This chapter scans most of the North American literature on applied ethics in adult education to show how the field has addressed ethics and where things stand as of 2009. Developments have occurred in two key areas: codes of ethics and ethical decision-making models.

Why Ethics Matters

On the front page of the May 26, 1991, *New York Times,* an article began with the headline "Students in a class on investments say the lessons meant big losses" (Henriques, 1991). This story became known in the field as "the Miami Case" and generated a great deal of anxiety among administrators responsible for adult education programs. In a nutshell, the story was about a class on the basics of investing offered by the Dade County (Florida) School District's adult education program. The instructor for the course was a broker employed by a Wall Street investment firm. The instructor won the confidence of the students to the point where they invested large sums of money with him, but they claimed that he placed those funds in riskier investments than they had agreed to. When their investments dropped substantially in value, they sued the instructor, his firm, and most notably the Dade County School District. The students accused the school system "of negligence in failing to supervise what was going on in [the instructor's] classes" and claimed that "selling investments to students violated both state law and codes of ethics" (p. 26). This case raised fundamental questions about the obligations of providers concerning "commercial" relationships that develop between students and instructors in adult education courses. The practice of hiring "experts" from business and industry to teach adult education classes is widespread and most often works to the advantage of all concerned. But this case raised questions about the ethics of commercial relationships that develop between adult learners and instructors and the obligations of providers to protect the financial and other interests of students.

The Miami Case spawned several initiatives. For example, the Learning Resources Network (LERN, 1992) developed *Industry Standards for Classes with Potential Commercial Content* to guide administrators in processes to avoid conflicts of interest. But the more significant impact was the general anxiety the case generated among adult educators about their moral and legal obligations to learners. The issues raised by this case were not new, but it was a wake-up call to adult educators about their ethical and legal obligations to learners.

Codes of Ethics

Developing and enforcing a code of ethics has long been considered a hallmark of self-regulating professions. Society grants certain privileges to the professions—for example, to decide who can enter the profession, what fees will be charged, and what training qualifies someone to practice—and in return the professions provide valuable services to society and protect the public from abuses of power and incompetence. But adult education has developed more as a field of practice than a profession, and there is continuing debate about whether any further "professionalization" of the field is desirable. It is what occupational sociologists might call a semiprofession while others prefer to think of adult education more as a calling or vocation (Collins, 1991).

There has been spirited debate in the literature about the desirability and feasibility of a code of ethics for adult education, and at least two published empirical studies of practitioner views. While this debate was under way, several organizations adopted codes of ethics and individuals have proposed others. As will be seen below, some of these codes are highly problematic and reinforce the arguments of those who oppose further professionalization of the field.

Many participants in the debate refer to a provocative observation made by Singarella and Sork (1983): "We doubt that the field of adult education is mature enough to reach agreement on a code of ethics which would apply to all practitioners. Further, we are not convinced that such a code would be desirable. Yet we are convinced that a thorough and ongoing exploration of ethical issues is essential to the continued growth and development of the field" (p. 250). This ambivalence reflected our recognition of the diversity of adult education practice and the lack of agreement on whether further professionalization was desirable. In 1988, Carlson enlivened the debate by publishing a strong critique of moves to further professionalize the field and any proposals to develop a code of ethics. He concluded, "There is no need to develop a professional code of ethics. Indeed, considerable evidence suggests advantage in avoiding this move. What is needed is a recognition of the choices facing us and a will to base these personal choices on reasoned and humane values" (Carlson, 1988, pp. 175–176). Other participants in the debate include Boulmetis and Russo (1991); Connelly and Light (1991); Cunningham (1992); Freeman, Shaeffer, and Whitson (1993); Griffith (1991); Hatcher and Storberg-Walker (2004); Ianinska and Garcia-Zamor (2006); Siegel (2000); Sork and Welock (1992); and Wood (1996).

Absent from the early arguments was any empirical evidence as to how practitioners felt about both the ethics of practice and codes of ethics. Knudson (1979) conducted a survey of professors of adult education as part of his unpublished doctoral dissertation. He was interested in identifying unethical situations that adult educators might encounter, with the goal of developing some useful guidelines to resolve them. Barber (1990) surveyed cooperative extension personnel about ethical issues they confront, again in an unpublished dissertation. McDonald and Wood (1993) reported on a survey of several groups of adult education practitioners in Indiana. Their study revealed a range of ethical issues that were of concern and a supportive attitude—among 52 percent of respondents (*n* = 249)—toward the need for a code of ethics. In an approximate replication of this study conducted in British Columbia, Gordon and Sork (2001) reported similar concerns about ethical issues and even stronger support—among 73 percent of respondents (*n* = 261)—of the need for a code of ethics. The issues, concerns, and dilemmas identified in the B.C. study fell into these categories, in decreasing order of frequency, which roughly parallel the findings of McDonald and Wood:

- Confidentiality
- Learner–adult educator relationship
- Finance
- Professionalism and competence
- Conflicts of interest
- Evaluating student performance
- Ownership of instructional materials
- Intraorganizational concerns
- Credentials
- Unsound training design
- Employment practices
- Enrolment and attendance (Gordon and Sork, 2001)

While the debate about the desirability of a code of ethics continued, several organizations and individuals were developing codes. The earliest I found was the *Statement of Ethics* by the Pennsylvania Association for Adult Continuing Education (PAACE, 1985). Michigan Adult and Community Educators followed by adopting a *Professional Code of Ethics* in 1992 (Mallet, 1994), the same year that the Learning Resources Network (LERN, 1992) issued its *Standards for Classes with Potential Commercial Content*—not quite a code of ethics but certainly a response to the legal and ethical issues raised by the Miami Case. One of the standards reads: "The program and its administration are not responsible for any activities that take place outside of the class between teachers and participants," which seems to be a clear reference to the Miami Case. In 1993, the Coalition of Adult Education Organizations (CAEO, now the Coalition of Lifelong Learning Organizations or COLLO) issued *Guidelines for Developing and Implementing a Code of Ethics for Adult Educators* (CAEO, 1993). According to David Stewart (1992), who led the effort to develop the *Guidelines,* they were released as a resource that adult education organizations could use to develop codes for their members. The *Guidelines* contains thirty-six clauses, one of which also seems directly related to the Miami Case. Clause 29 reads: "Class time is not used to sell a product or service or to distribute flyers or business cards that are oriented to the financial interests of an instructor or program leader (unless the *explicit* and pre-announced purposes of the class include that of explaining a product or service with the objective of encouraging sales)" (p. 4).

New Directions for Adult and Continuing Education • DOI: 10.1002/ace

The Learning Resources Network's *Code of Ethics* (LERN, 1994) contains clauses directed to three groups: administrators, teachers, and learners. This is odd, because codes of ethics are usually developed to protect the less powerful (learners) from the more powerful (administrators or teachers). So it is highly unusual for an organization of providers to stipulate what is ethical for those they serve. In a sense, this is equivalent to a lawyer's code of ethics stipulating norms of behavior for their clients.

In 1995, the Singapore Association for Continuing Education (SACE) adopted its *Code of Ethics* with five clauses beginning with "The Adult Educator adheres to the laws and regulations governing the organising of programmes." This opening clause has parallels in other codes and suggests a concern with being lawful (Sork, 1996). As Gordon and Sork (2001) observed:

> It is troubling to note that some of the codes of ethics that have been produced for adult education contain clauses that call for "following existing rules, policies and laws." These clauses would effectively render unethical the work of social activists such as Paulo Freire and Miles Horton [and various feminist and popular educators], who deliberately broke rules, policies and laws that were unjust and oppressive [p. 215].

Although it is understandable why some professional organizations want to encourage members to practice in a lawful way—and to "excommunicate" them if found guilty of an egregious violation of criminal or civil law—such clauses reinforce the criticism that codes privilege those in power and make it difficult to engage in work that challenges the status quo (Sork, 1996).

Wood's "framework for reflecting on ethical issues in adult education" (1996) contains nine clauses. Even given the diversity of adult education, Wood believed that the nine "responsibilities" he argued that adult educators have are more or less universal for those in Western, democratic societies. His "contention . . . is that the framework . . . is the sort of code that the profession should have, that it is applicable across all program areas in the field, and that the elements of the framework are appropriate, not that the code is perfect" (p. 14).

The Association for Continuing Higher Education (ACHE) published its *Code of Ethics* in 1997 after a consultative process including surveys of members (Lawler, 1996, 2000a). This single-page, eight-clause code addresses program quality, fair and equal access, conflicts of interest, confidentiality, best practices, impact of policies, truth in advertising, and fiscal responsibility.

At the other extreme, we have what is to date the most elaborate and ambitious code from the Academy of Human Resource Development (AHRD): *Standards on Ethics and Integrity* (1999). This comprehensive document includes sections on general standards, research and evaluation, advertising and other public statements, publication of work, privacy and confidentiality, teaching and facilitating, and resolution of ethical issues and violations.

According to the authors:

> These Standards on Ethics and Integrity for the Academy of Human Resource Development provide guidance for HRD professionals engaged in practice, research, consulting, and instruction/facilitation/teaching. Although these principles are aspirational in nature, they provide standards of conduct and set forth a common set of values for HRD professionals. Adherence to these standards builds ethical, professional, and research accomplishments for HRD professionals and adds to the further definition and clarification of HRD as a profession. The primary goal of these standards is to define more clearly a holistic balance among individuals, groups, organizations, communities, and societies whenever conflicting needs arise [AHRD, 1999, p. 1].

The American Society for Training and Development (ASTD) has a *Code of Ethics* that predates the AHRD code, although the date of its original publication is unclear. The eleven-clause ASTD code:

> provides guidance to individuals to be self-managed workplace learning and performance professionals. Clients and employers should expect the highest possible standards of personal integrity, professional competence, sound judgment and discretion. Developed by the profession for the profession, the Code of Ethics is the public declaration of workplace learning and performance professionals' obligations to themselves, their profession, and society [ASTD, 2008].

The most recently developed code I have found is the one proposed by Siegel (2000) and based on a broad review of the literature including the work done by ACHE. Siegel believes that it is desirable and feasible to develop a "universal" code of ethics and builds on the ACHE code to expand its scope beyond continuing higher education. He stipulates ten principles that should be included in a universal code, saying that adult educators should:

1. Utilize, to the extent possible, the best available professional knowledge and practices in serving all learners.
2. Respect the ethno-socio-cultural heritage, special circumstances, and dignity as human beings of all adult learners.
3. Avoid conflicts of interest, or the appearance of conflicts of interest, in all aspects of their work.
4. Respect and strive to ensure as appropriate the need for confidentiality of each learner in interactions between learner and educator.
5. Respect the unique and diverse learning needs of adult learners; should respect the need of each learner for honesty, understanding,

and fairness; should respect the real or perceived disparity in position between educator and learner; and should respect the right of learners to participate in any solutions designed to meet their needs.

6. Be cognizant of, remain sensitive to, and communicate the real or perceived negative impact of institutional or organizational policies and procedures on the learners, the institution or organization, and the community as a whole.

7. Present advertising information concerning services and programs that is clear, complete, accurate, and descriptive of the actual services and programs being offered.

8. Present services and programs that are fiscally responsible to all stakeholders, with results based upon objective and honest assessment.

9. Assist in empowering learners to participate actively and effectively to improve the general welfare of their immediate and global communities and to promote the concepts of a just and equitable society.

10. Avoid doing any harm to learners [pp. 52–57].

After reviewing the arguments for and against codes of ethics and the extensive work done on developing or proposing codes for a variety of adult education contexts, what are we left with for 2009 and beyond? I believe that it is a much more refined understanding of the issues and how challenging it is to think about having a code of ethics that would be relevant to most practitioners, regardless of context. This development doesn't even address the problems of where such a code would be located and if or how its provisions would be enforced.

Although I have participated on the "pro" side of the debate about codes of ethics, I remain ambivalent, as I was in 1983 (Singarella and Sork, 1983), about whether it is possible or desirable for adult education to develop and adopt a widely accepted code of ethics. I suspect that organizations may also be ambivalent about codes of ethics; some that developed codes do not currently make them available on their websites (for example, Association for Continuing Higher Education, Learning Resources Network, Coalition of Adult Education Organizations and Coalition of Lifelong Learning Organizations, Pennsylvania Association for Adult Continuing Education).

Codes—even proposed codes—can be useful tools to engage practitioners and students in conversations about the moral dimensions of practice and what aspects of practice are most likely to be ethically sensitive. Critically analyzing clauses in a code of ethics—like the ones in Siegel's code above—can help us understand the values that underlie the field and some of the morally hazardous terrain we traverse in our day-to-day practice. But the absence of a code is no excuse to ignore the ethical dimensions of practice, because there are other tools available to help us understand this aspect of our work. One is ethical decision-making frameworks.

Ethical Decision Making

Many adult educators have tried to develop more or less systematic processes to help practitioners reason their way to sound ethical choices. I developed the Ethical Practices Analysis (Sork, 1990), designed to reveal the ethical arguments used to justify or refute common practices. Brockett (1988b) proposed a broad model of ethical practice that included three dimensions: personal value system, consideration of multiple responsibilities, and operationalization of values. It was "intended to serve as a tentative guide for understanding a process that can be used by educators of adults in ethical decision making and for clarifying some of the types of questions that need to be asked when examining ethical issues" (pp. 13–14). Zinn (1993) offered a nine-step process for making ethical decisions, including the less rational but helpful advice to "trust your heart" (or moral intuition) and to "sleep on it." Gordon (1993) used the metaphor of "peeling onions" to discuss solving moral dilemmas. She suggested that we must peel our own multilayered onion down to our ethical core as well as getting to the core of multilayered ethical dilemmas.

Brockett and Hiemstra (2004) propose an ethical decision-making (EDM) model that uses a set of questions linked to values, obligations, and consequences to guide decision making. Their questions are:

- What do I believe? About human nature? About the education of adults? About ethics?
- How committed am I to the beliefs I hold?
- Which basic values drive my practice?
- To whom am I responsible?
- To what extent does an ethical dilemma result from conflicting obligations?
- What are my options?
- What are the possible consequences of my actions?
- Which option is most consistent with my values? [p. 17]

Like multistep decision models, these questions provide a general framework for thinking through a complex issue with no easy resolution. However, they don't challenge me to question my own values or give me any basis for evaluating the best course of action except its consistency with my values. Acting consistently with one's values can be virtuous but only if the values themselves constitute a coherent, defensible foundation for practice.

I have used in my teaching a framework proposed by Nash (2002) and found it more demanding than most other frameworks but also more helpful in thinking through complex issues for which there might be several possible courses of action. He proposes the development of a "third language moral brief" "as a preliminary to constructing a sound defense for taking a particular ethical action" (p. 117). Nash believes that only a "thin

moral language" is capable of resolving moral dilemmas in a secular plural-
ist society, and the third language he proposes is "thin" because "it relies not
on specific familial, religious, political, or metaphysical accounts of moral-
ity, but on abstract, general, and principled accounts, set within . . . formal
constraints of tolerance, mutual respect, and rights of self-determination"
(p. 110).

What I find most useful from this framework is a set of questions he
proposes as scaffolding for the moral brief*:

1.   Why is this case a moral dilemma?
2.   What are the choices in conflict?
3.   Who are the morally relevant actors?
4.   Where does the action take place? Is the "where" morally relevant?
5.   When does the action take place? Is the "when" morally relevant?
6.   How is the manner or style of action morally relevant?
7.   What are some foreseeable consequences of each decision?
8.   What are some foreseeable principles involved in each decision?
9.   What are some viable alternatives?
10   What does the code of ethics say?
11   What is your decision? [p. 117]

After answering these questions, he then suggests developing a "justification schema," which is "a step-by-step, principled defense of a particular ethical decision [or course of action]" (pp. 128–129). The schema
consists of answers to these questions*:

1.   What is your decision A? What is your decision B? [Where A and B
     represent alternatives under consideration in no particular order of
     preference]
2.   What *rules* do you appeal to in order to justify (support, give reasons
     for) each of the decisions?
3.   What *principles* do you appeal to in order to justify each of the
     decisions?
4.   What *theories* do you appeal to in order to justify each of the
     decisions?
5.   What conclusions do you reach regarding your final decision after
     you compare both justifications?
6.   What afterthoughts do you have now that you have made your final
     decision? [p. 129]

The underlying rationale for proposing these tools for ethical decision
making is that the issues are often complex, the alternative courses of action

* Reprinted with permission of the Publisher. From Robert J. Nash, *"Real World" Ethics: Frameworks for Educators and Human Service Professionals.* New York: Teachers College Press. Copyright
(c) 2002 by Teachers College, Columbia University. All rights reserved.

unclear, and the factors to be considered multifaceted, so practitioners may value a more systematic approach. The assumption is that by approaching the task systematically and mindfully a more defensible decision will be reached. Although it is possible to rely exclusively on our moral intuition and gut feelings to arrive at right actions, they do not contribute to development of a moral community in which there exists a more or less common frame of reference for determining right actions. That may be an unachievable ideal in adult education, but it is a goal I hope will be pursued by others as the field evolves.

Concluding Observations

Each time I take a fresh look at developments in ethics in adult and continuing education, I am both heartened and discouraged. I am heartened by the earnest efforts being made by some to keep the ethics of practice visible and part of the ongoing professional development of practitioners. In the few surveys that have been conducted, practitioners seem to be asking for help with this aspect of their work, so continuing attention to this is warranted. I am discouraged by the absence—or superficial treatment—of ethics in much of the adult education literature. It seems as if many in the field view our work as inherently virtuous or morally harmless and therefore not subject to the same kind of critical ethical analysis as other occupations. This is not only wrong but also dangerous.

As is the case with most bodies of literature dealing with adult and continuing education, a Euro-Western perspective dominates the area of applied ethics and a Western form of rationality and Western values characterize efforts to develop codes of ethics and frameworks for making decisions. In a globalizing world where diversity is a key feature, there are limits to approaches anchored in one philosophical tradition that privileges a certain set of values. It is hard to predict the direction this aspect of adult education will take in the years ahead. But what does seem clear is that the moral dimensions of practice will become even more complex as concerns about the environment, inclusion, respect, and diversity interact with changes in technology, the economy, and emerging institutional forms in adult and continuing education.

It is the best of times and the worst of times to be an adult educator. It is the best because of the dizzying array of choices available for organizing and delivering learning experiences—and for adults to pursue learning independently using the Web and other resources. It is the worst because of escalating expectations the public has for the quality, convenience, timeliness, and relevance of programs we offer. There are some potentially useful tools available to help us with the difficult ethical choices that lie ahead. It remains to be seen if they—and we—are up to the challenge of meeting these expectations in a morally defensible way.

New Directions for Adult and Continuing Education • DOI: 10.1002/ace

References

Academy of Human Resource Development (AHRD), Standing Committee on Ethics and Integrity. *AHRD Standards on Ethics and Integrity,* First Edition, May 1999. (http://www.ahrd.org/mc/page.do?sitePageId=56727andorgId=ahrd).

American Association for Adult and Continuing Education. Special issue of *Adult Learning,* Nov./Dec. 1993, 5(2).

American Society for Training and Development. *Code of Ethics.* Retrieved December 20, 2008, from http://www.astd.org/ASTD/aboutus/missionAndVision/.

Barber, S. L. "Ethical Issues and Perceptions of Importance and Frequency by Adult Educators in the Cooperative Extension System." *Dissertation Abstracts International,* 50(1), 1990, 3445 A.

Boulmetis, J., and Russo, F. X. "A Question of Ethics." *Community Education Journal,* 1991, 18(2), 15–18.

Brockett, R. G. (ed.). *Ethical Issues in Adult Education.* New York: Teachers College Press, 1988a.

Brockett, R. G. "Ethics and the Adult Educator." In R. G. Brockett (ed.), *Ethical Issues in Adult Education.* New York: Teachers College Press, 1988b, pp. 1–16.

Brockett, R. G., and Hiemstra, R. "Philosophical and Ethical Considerations." In P. S. Cookson (ed.), *Program Planning for the Training and Continuing Education of Adults: North American Perspectives.* Malabar, Fla.: Krieger, 1998.

Brockett, R. G., and Hiemstra, R. *Toward Ethical Practice.* Malabar, Fla.: Krieger, 2004.

Brookfield, S. "Ethical Issues in Evaluating Adult Education Programs." In R. G. Brockett (ed.), *Ethical Issues in Adult Education.* New York: Teachers College Press, 1988.

Burge, E. J. (ed.). Special issue of *Open Learning,* 22(2), 2007.

Burns, J. H., and Roche, G. A. "Marketing for Adult Educators: Some Ethical Questions." In R. G. Brockett (ed.), *Ethical Issues in Adult Education.* New York: Teachers College Press, 1988.

Caffarella, R. S. *Planning Programs for Adult Learners: A Practical Guide for Educators, Trainers and Staff Developers* (2nd ed). San Francisco: Jossey-Bass, 2002.

Carlson, R. A. (1988). "A Code of Ethics for Adult Educators?" In R. G. Brockett (ed.), *Ethical Issues in Adult Education.* New York: Teachers College Press, 1988.

Cervero, R. M., and Wilson, A. L. *Planning Responsibly for Adult Education: A Guide to Negotiating Power and Interests.* San Francisco: Jossey-Bass, 1994.

Cervero, R. M., and Wilson, A. L. *Working the Planning Table: Negotiating Democratically for Adult, Continuing, and Workplace Education.* San Francisco: Jossey-Bass, 2006.

Coalition of Adult Education Organizations (CAEO; now Coalition of Lifelong Learning Organizations). *Guidelines for Developing and Implementing a Code of Ethics for Adult Educators.* Adopted by board of directors of CAEO, June 11, 1993.

Collins, M. *Adult Education as Vocation: A Critical Role for the Adult Educator.* New York: Routledge, 1991.

Connelly, R. J., and Light, K. M. "An Interdisciplinary Code of Ethics for Adult Education." *Adult Education Quarterly,* 1991, 41(4), 233–240.

Cunningham, P. M. "Adult and Continuing Education Does Not Need a Code of Ethics." In B. R. Sisco and M. W. Galbraith (eds.), *Confronting Controversies in Challenging Times: A Call to Action.* New Directions for Adult and Continuing Education, no. 54. San Francisco: Jossey-Bass, 1992.

Elias, J. L., and Merriam, S. B. *Philosophical Foundations of Adult Education* (3rd ed.). Malabar, Fla.: Krieger, 2005.

Felch, W. C. "Ethics and Continuing Medical Education." *Mobius,* 1986, 6(1), 80–85.

Freeman, M. K., Shaeffer, J. M., and Whitson, D. L. "Ethical Practice Contributes to Professionalization in Adult and Continuing Education: The Debate Continues." *Adult Learning,* 1993, 5(2), 9–10.

Galbraith, M. W., Sisco, B. R., and Guglielmino, L. M. *Administering Successful Programs for Adults: Promoting Excellence in Adult, Community and Continuing Education.* Malabar, Fla.: Krieger, 1997.

Gordon, J. C. "Peeling Onions: Some Tools and a Recipe for Solving Ethical Dilemmas." *Adult Learning,* 1993, *5*(2), 11–12, 24.

Gordon, W., and Sork, T. J. "Ethical Issues and Codes of Ethics: Views of Adult Education Practitioners in Canada and the US." *Adult Education Quarterly,* 2001, *51*(3), 202–218.

Griffith, W. S. "Do Adult Educators Need a Code of Ethics?" *Adult Learning,* 1991, *2*(8), 4.

Hatcher, T., and Storberg-Walker, J. "Developing Ethical Adult Educators: A Re-examination of the Need for a Code of Ethics." *Adult Learning,* 2004, *14*(2), 21–24.

Henriques, D. B. "Students in a Class on Investments Say the Lessons Meant Big Losses." *New York Times,* May 26, 1991, pp. 1, 26.

Holt, M. E. "Adult Educators in Cyberspace: Ethical Considerations." *Adult Learning.* 1996, *8*(2), 15–16, 25.

Holt, M. E. "Ethical Considerations in Internet-based Adult Education." In B. Cahoon (ed.), *Adult Learning and the Internet.* New Directions for Adult and Continuing Education, no. 78. San Francisco: Jossey-Bass, 1998.

Ianinska, S., and Garcia-Zamor, J.-C. (2006). "Morals, Ethics, and Integrity: How Codes of Conduct Contribute to Ethical Adult Education Practice." *Public Organization Review,* 2006, 6, 3–20.

Jarvis, P. *Ethics and Education for Adults in a Late Modern Society.* Leicester: National Institute for Adult and Continuing Education (England and Wales), 1997.

Johnson, W. B., and Ridley, C. R. (2008). *The Elements of Ethics for Professionals.* New York: Palgrave Macmillan.

Knudson, R. S. *A Philosophical Analysis of* The Flies *with Ethical Implications for Adult Education.* Unpublished doctoral dissertation. University of Wisconsin-Madison, 1979.

Lawler, P. A. "Developing a Code of Ethics: A Case Study Approach." *Journal of Continuing Higher Education,* 1996, *44*(3), 2–14.

Lawler, P. A. "The ACHE Code of Ethics: Its Role for the Profession." *Journal of Continuing Higher Education,* 2000a, *48*(3), 31–34.

Lawler, P. A. "Ethical Issues in Continuing Professional Education." In V. W. Mott and B. J. Daley (eds.), *Charting a Course for Continuing Professional Education: Reframing Professional Practice.* New Directions for Adult and Continuing Education, no. 86. San Francisco: Jossey-Bass, 2000b.

Lawler, P. A. "Ethics and Continuing Professional Education: Today's Challenges, Tomorrow's Solutions." *Adult Learning,* 2001, *12*(1), 18–19.

Lawler, P. A., and Fielder, J. "Ethical Problems in Continuing Higher Education: Results of a Survey." *Journal of Continuing Higher Education,* 1993, *41*(1), 25–33.

Lawson, K. H. *Philosophical Concepts and Values in Adult Education* (rev. ed.). Milton Keynes, UK: Open University Press, 1979.

Lawson, K. H. "Philosophy and Ethics in Adult Education." In A. C. Tuijnman (ed.), *International Encyclopedia of Adult Education and Training* (2nd ed.). Oxford, UK: Pergamon, 1996.

Learning Resources Network (LERN). *Industry Standards for Classes with Potential Commercial Content.* Recommendations from the Blue Ribbon Committee on Industry Standards of the Learning Resources Network. *Adult and Continuing Education Today,* 22(24), June 22, 1992.

Learning Resources Network (LERN). *Learning Resources Network Code of Ethics.* Manhattan, Kan.: Learning Resources Network, 1994.

Lenz, E. *The Art of Teaching Adults.* New York: Holt, Rinehart and Winston, 1982.

Maidment, R., and Losito, W. F. *Ethics and Professional Trainers*. Madison, Wis.: American Society for Training and Development. (ERIC Document Reproduction Service No. ED 186 980), 1980.

Mallet, R. H. "Quality Means Being Ethical." *Adult Learning*, 1994, 5(6), 13–14.

Martel, L. D., and Colley, R. M. "Ethical Issues in Marketing and Continuing Education." In H. Beder (ed.), *Marketing Continuing Education*. New Directions for Continuing Education, no. 31. San Francisco: Jossey-Bass, 1986.

McDonald, K. S., and Wood, G. S., Jr. "Surveying Adult Education Practitioners About Ethical Issues." *Adult Education Quarterly*, 1993, 43(4), 243–257.

Michigan Adult and Community Educators. *Adult and Community Education Professional Code of Ethics*. 1992. See http://www.michigan.gov/mde.

Nash, R. J. *"Real World" Ethics: Frameworks for Educators and Human Service Professionals* (2nd ed.). New York: Teachers College Press, 2002.

Pearson, G. A., and Kennedy, M. S. "Business Ethics: Implications for Providers and Faculty of Continuing Education." *Journal of Continuing Education in Nursing*, 1985, 16(1), 4–6.

Pennsylvania Association for Adult Continuing Education (PAACE). *Statement of Ethics*. 1985. See http://www.paacesite.org/.

Pratt, D. D. "Ethical Reasoning in Teaching Adults". In M. W. Galbraith (ed.), *Adult Learning Methods: A Guide for Effective Instruction*. Malabar, Fla.: Krieger, 1998.

Price, D. W. "Ethical Dilemmas in Administrative Practice." *Adult Learning*, 1997, 9(1), 15–17.

Reed, D., and Sork, T. J. "Ethical Considerations in Distance Education." *American Journal of Distance Education*, 1990, 4(2), 30–43.

Scanlan, C. L. "Ethical Issues in Continuing Professional Education." In R. M. Cervero and C. L. Scanlan (eds.), *Problems and Prospects in Continuing Professional Education*. New Directions for Continuing Education, no. 27. San Francisco: Jossey-Bass, 1985.

Siegel, I. S. "Toward Developing a Universal Code of Ethics for Adult Educators." *PAACE Journal of Lifelong Learning*, 2000, 9, 39–64. See http://www.coe.iup.edu/ace/volume_9.html.

Singapore Association for Continuing Education (SACE). *Singapore Association for Continuing Education Code of Ethics*. Singapore: SACE, 1995. See http://www.spc.org.sg/member/saceh1.htm.

Singarella, T. A., and Sork, T. J. "Questions of Value and Conduct: Ethical Issues for Adult Education." *Adult Education Quarterly*, 1983, 33(4), 244–251.

Sisco, B. R. "Dilemmas in Continuing Education Administration." In R. G. Brockett (ed.), *Ethical Issues in Adult Education*. New York: Teachers College Press, 1988.

Sork, T. J. "Ethical Issues in Program Planning." In R. G. Brockett (ed.), *Ethical Issues in Adult Education*. New York: Teachers College Press, 1988.

Sork, T. J. "An 'Ethical Practices Analysis' for Adult Educators." Paper presented at the annual conference of the American Association for Adult and Continuing Education, Salt Lake City, Oct. 1990.

Sork, T. J. "A Few Potholes on the Road to Salvation: Codes of Ethics in Adult Education." *Proceedings of the 37th Annual Adult Education Research Conference*, May 16–19, 1996. Tampa: University of South Florida.

Sork, T. J. "Planning Educational Programs." In A. L. Wilson and E. R. Hayes (eds.), *Handbook of Adult and Continuing Education*. San Francisco: Jossey-Bass, 2000.

Sork, T. J. "Ethics." In L. M. English (ed.), *International Encyclopedia of Adult Education*. Houndmills, UK: Palgrave Macmillan, 2005.

Sork, T. J., and Welock, B. A. "Adult and Continuing Education Needs a Code of Ethics." In B. R. Sisco and M. W. Galbraith (eds.), *Confronting Controversies in Challenging Times: A Call to Action*. New Directions for Adult and Continuing Education, no. 54. San Francisco: Jossey-Bass, 1992.

Stewart, D. "It's Time to Get Serious About a Code of Ethics for Adult Educators." *Adult and Continuing Education Today,* 1992, 2(4).

Tarrant, J. "The Ethics of Post-compulsory Education and Training in a Democracy." *Journal of Further and Higher Education,* 2001, 25(3), 369–378.

Weston, A. *A Practical Companion to Ethics* (3rd ed.). Oxford: Oxford University Press, 2005.

Wilson, A. L., and Cervero, R. M. "Who Sits at the Planning Table: Ethics and Planning Practice." *Adult Learning,* 1996, 8(2), 20–22.

Wood, G. S., Jr. "A Code of Ethics for All Adult Educators?" *Adult Learning,* 1996, 8(2), 13–14.

Zinn, L. M. "Do the Right Thing: Ethical Decision-Making in Professional and Business Practice." *Adult Learning,* 1993, 5(2), 7–8; 27.

THOMAS J. SORK is professor of adult education and associate dean of external programs and learning technologies in the Faculty of Education at the University of British Columbia in Canada.

3

*This chapter describes a number of ethical dilemmas
faced as a workplace literacy practitioner and researcher.
Each issue is analyzed along with the lessons learned.*

Workplace Literacy: Ethical Issues
Through the Lens of Experience

Sue Folinsbee

Since the mid-1980s, my work as a practitioner and researcher has focused
on education in the workplace, including literacy development. By "literacy
development," I refer to programs that focus on basic skills such as document use, writing, math, communications, and computers, usually but not
always for those workers without a high school diploma or much postsec-
ondary education. As a practitioner, I have worked with employers, unions,
and other partners to plan and set up "workplace literacy programs" as well
as mentoring and providing professional development for other workplace
educators. As a researcher, I spent six months on the factory floor to conduct an ethnographic study of how workers and management use literacy
(or not) in a textile factory.

As a novice workplace practitioner, my understanding that the workplace is a contested terrain was immediate, although how to work with its
complexities was not. Over time, my understanding of how to work with
the complexities of this contested terrain became much deeper, but it is still
a work in progress. Even though principles to guide practice are crucial,
there are no hard-and-fast rules for resolving ethical issues—dilemmas that
are not easily resolvable because they present opposing values and outcomes
that may do harm to certain groups of people if not properly considered.

Note: I thank Mary Ellen Belfiore and Lynette Plett for reviewing earlier drafts of this
chapter.

When I enter a workplace, I have a code of conduct in my head, a set of principles that I hope to follow. In the beginning, I developed this code from reading about the work of colleagues, reading academic literature, talking to peers, reflecting, and mulling things over. The principles help me make decisions that are consistent and thoughtful and that set limits about when to say no (Steel, Johnston, Folinsbee, and Belfiore, 1997). They are worker-centered, having at their core a respect for workers, the jobs they do, how they learn, and what might or might not be in their interests.

My main principles are ensuring worker and management commitment to a workplace education initiative, confidentiality, joint planning to get a clear understanding of the differing interests throughout the context, a holistic, asset-based approach, and voluntary participation. Over time, this code has become seasoned and nuanced with experience, but the basic tenets remain the same, if not stronger. I also rely on my intuition to warn me about potential ethical issues: when I have a "pit" in my stomach I know there is a dilemma that I need to pay attention to and resolve. When I avoid paying attention, negative consequences arise. Sork (1988) stresses the importance of having a personal philosophy so that one has a basis for resolving the ethical dilemmas of practice. While indicating that practitioners make evaluative judgments all the time, he stresses the importance of the ethics of practice so that decisions are made consciously—recognizing their value base and their consequences.

Encountering and grappling with ethical dilemmas is a necessary component of workplace literacy practice. However, such dilemmas, especially when they are not resolved successfully, are not usually discussed in the professional literature or public presentations. In my own work, I usually reserve these conversations for debriefings with my most trusted colleagues. I've learned that the most important teachers for my colleagues were not only the successful initiatives but also the ones that were not so successful (Folinsbee, 2000). One model has helped me think about my own praxis.

The Spiral Model

Arnold and others (1991) developed the Spiral Model to help practitioners work with the tensions between practice and theory in workshops and educational programs. The model begins with the experience of participants, moves to looking for patterns in that experience, and then generates new information or theory on the basis of these patterns. Next, participants practice skills and devise strategies for action, leading to actual applied action. Using this model as a framework for an analysis of my own learning, I start with my own experience and that of trusted peers. I work with what I know to be true from that collective, my own individual experience, and the body of professional literature. With each new personal experience, peers insights, and reading, I add new information and theory and adjust and expand my

New Directions for Adult and Continuing Education • DOI: 10.1002/ace

repertoire of how to work with all the conflicting ethical factors and dynamics in workplace literacy development.

For example, I used to think that conducting a formal organizational needs assessment was *de rigueur* (Folinsbee and Jurmo, 1994). It would be imperative to understand the perspectives of all stakeholders in order to properly understand the organizational context and its real needs. Otherwise how could I determine any levels of support for a workplace literacy program? or define program policy and parameters? Belfiore (2002), for example, found that in all the statements of good program planning practice she reviewed, an organizational or workplace needs assessment was seen as a necessary step in the planning process for a workplace basic skills program; it enabled the voices from all levels of the workforce to be heard regarding their views on a possible program.

However, I have learned from practice that there is the odd case when conducting a formal organizational needs assessment may not be the most expedient or effective strategy. For example, in one municipal workplace, a new, mandatory certification test had been legislated for certain job classifications. All employees in the designated job classifications had to pass different provincially mandated exams. Some workers had been unable to pass the exam, even though they knew how to do the job well and had worked in it for years. As a result of the exam failure, they were at risk of losing their jobs. Both the union and management recognized that these workers needed some support in document use, math, and test taking to prepare to retake the test. All agreed on the organizational need, and time was of the essence. Assessing the organizational context meant, for me, talking to management and labor representatives and then going straight into a confidential, individual needs assessment process to understand where these workers needed specific upgrading support for taking the test again and passing. I found that this was a viable strategy for this kind of situation. On the basis of this experience, I adjusted my thinking to consider the occasional situations when a formal organizational needs analysis might not be required. These kinds of experiences—where one must adjust one's thinking about what principles mean in practice—remind us that even though principles remain steadfast, the practice we engage in needs to be flexible.

So join me on a journey through three of the most difficult ethical dilemmas I have faced over the past twenty or so years. Some details are changed to protect the confidentiality of those involved. The first case takes place within a financial institution, the second at a newspaper, and the third in a plastics factory.

Financial Institution: Writing Not the Issue

I was invited into a financial institution by a manager who told me that he knew the five employees who needed a literacy program and that he also knew exactly what they needed: Could I, immediately, develop a writing program for these employees so they could improve their spelling and grammar and write better reports? Now, I felt an ethical dilemma because the needs were entirely employer-defined. I convinced the manager that I should do a small organizational analysis to understand the issue better and make sure I was "offering the best solution" to the company. He agreed, so I interviewed the five workers, their co-workers, supervisors, and managers in the relevant department.

The workers in fact did not need a writing course; their highest priority issue was improved communication between the workers and their supervisors. The company scrapped the idea of the writing program and instead concentrated on strategies to improve relations between supervisors and workers in the department. Had I listened to only one slice of the pie and offered a strategy based on one manager's perspective, I would have given a solution in no one's best interests, and certainly not the workers facing enforced participation in what to them was an irrelevant program. The more pressing problems identified by the workers would have kept bubbling away under the surface despite any quick fix program. After all this action, on reflection, where were the ethical issues?

Serving Interests. This case raises the first issue. Who is the client? Whose interests do we serve as workplace educators? We may have to work with all the interests held by the levels of management and workers, along with funders' and educators' own institutional interests. For me, at the heart of working with and balancing these interests lies a worker-centered approach: maintaining consistent respect for workers and their needs (Folinsbee, 2000). In this scenario, conducting a needs analysis served to uncover the perspectives of all the stakeholders and get to the heart of how they defined the real issue. I agree with Fiona Frank, a UK-based workplace educator, when she points out that it is "nice to think it's just the learners but someone else is paying the bill—the company, a local or national agency. We have to serve a lot of masters *and* keep our integrity" (Folinsbee, 2000, p. 6). Paul Jurmo also agrees with Frank when he argues, "Hard to say. As an adult educator I say the learner . . . but other people are investing money. Management and the union are interested stakeholders. Is a stakeholder a client? It is important to try to understand and serve all interests . . . find a focus of mutual interest" (p. 6). Tamara Levine, however, working in a Canadian labor organization, holds another view: "My role is to serve workers and their unions, although I don't think of them as clients. Sometimes I work with joint committees, but I am accountable to the union" (p. 6).

Power Relationships. How do I work with those uneven workplace power relationships? How do I work to even out those power relationships—a task inherent in my role as workplace educator? One way to even them out in planning is to work with a joint management-worker committee and conduct an organizational needs analysis to determine all the perceived needs, whether or not an education program is even the right solution, and how or where literacy fits. In this scenario, there was no committee but there was a needs analysis. On reflection, I am not sure that a committee would have been the best idea because there a certain urgency applied to the situation. It is imperative to contextualize our responses to a particular situation while staying grounded in our principles.

Understandings of Literacy. This situation also points to how I define literacy. Do I see literacy as a set of skills or tasks, or do I see literacy as embedded in social and cultural practices that are part of institutionalized systems (Belfiore and others, 2004; Connon-Unda, 2001)? That manager in the financial institution perceived literacy as a set of skills and tasks to "fix a problem." My own understandings of literacy—as social practice, as a thread in the workplace weave—and the idea of multiple literacies did not crystallize until I conducted research in a textile factory (Belfiore and others, 2004) to find out people's literacy practices within the cultural practices of their workplace. What dilemmas does defining literacy pose? A definition that focuses on discrete tasks and skills, especially those that just focus on the job, may suit what employers and funders want in a program and see as easily measurable in terms of accountability frameworks and measurable outcomes. However, focusing on isolated tasks and skills and leaving out the social context from the definition may address on-the-ground identified worker needs and management objectives only partially, if at all. On the other hand, how do I gain agreement and support from management and funders using a deeper, more holistic, more critical approach? Jean Connon-Unda (2001) therefore encourages me to answer the question "Literacy for what?" as fully as possible in relation to all aspects of workers' lives.

Mandatory Participation. Ideally, all participation in any kind of workplace education program is voluntary, not mandated by the employer (Belfiore, 2002). Applying mandatory participation in a workplace literacy program can create resistance and additional barriers for workers who may already have experienced education-based failure and marginalization. Initially, in this first scenario, certain workers had been singled out for mandatory participation by management. Fortunately, the organizational needs analysis shifted the focus from the skills of five employees to larger issues at play.

Curriculum. The organizational needs assessment, with individual goal setting with learners, determines what kinds of programs are desired by workers and management, as well as the circumstances under which they should occur. Workers may be interested in broader educational goals that go beyond their present jobs. Management may be interested in a program that focuses specifically on a job-related issue (as in this financial institution). For a successful outcome in workplace program offering and participation, program goals and content need to be carefully negotiated so that they meet workers' identified needs but also carry the overt commitment of management. Belfiore (2002) argues that workplace educators are responsible for clarifying to our stakeholders which kinds of programs can serve differing educational needs, interests, and expected outcomes.

New Directions for Adult and Continuing Education • DOI: 10.1002/ace

Promising Too Much. Overpromising the benefits and outcomes of a workplace literacy programs may get me into ethical trouble. If I had given a literacy program as requested by the manager and without an organizational needs analysis, both workers and management would have been frustrated with the outcomes. Either the program or the workers might then have been scapegoats when the program was not perceived as a success by management.

Education Institutional Expectations Versus Real Workplace Needs. The first scenario does not explicitly raise the issue of certain organizational demands on programming decisions, but I raise it here because you may already have encountered this problem. What happens to ethical decision making when the workplace educator's employer demands an annual revenue stream from a certain number of workplace programs? Some workplace educators live under constant pressure to get the numbers and run programs, as opposed to first doing an organizational scan, which may indicate need for a program the educator cannot fulfill, or conversely it may indicate no need at all for a revenue-generating program. Some workplace educators might have developed a program based on management's original assessment just to get the program and meet their own educational institution's expectations and interests. Similarly, independent contractors would be expecting to get the much needed program work. Others who work as workplace coordinators for government might feel pressure to implement a program whether it was feasible or not, just to get the numbers.

Basic Skills at a Newspaper: Employee Jobs at Risk

In a small city newspaper office, workers in proof reading were required to take a test by their employer "to determine their skills and their accuracy." As a result of this company-mandated test, fourteen workers passed and four failed. Those who failed became at risk of losing their jobs, unless they could improve their skills and their accuracy. A prominent board member connected to the newspaper called me into this very tense situation to help the four workers. I was working for a nonprofit literacy organization at the time. This particular board member was an employer who was a public champion for literacy and had worked for many years to support and advocate for adult literacy. I wanted to honor her request because her intentions were to support the workers in question and find a solution that would help them keep their jobs. In initial conversations with the newspaper's Human Resources Department, I was asked to individually test the workers' basic skills. I convinced the manager that the situation called for a small-scale organizational analysis and an interview with each of the four workers.

The organizational analysis showed us that anxiety and frustrations ran high for these workers, and that a large gap existed between union and management perspectives on the situation. The union was heartily opposed to the original test, its results, and the consequences of failing it. My discussions

New Directions for Adult and Continuing Education • DOI: 10.1002/ace

with the union revealed its nonnegotiable need to keep confidential any assessment results for an upgrading program; a principle with which I totally agreed. The HR manager reluctantly agreed to aggregate assessment results, not produce individual results. However, once the nine-week test program was put in motion, the HR manager reneged and put pressure on me and my co-worker (who conducted the needs analysis and designed the program) to produce individual results. My colleague and I remained firm that the program could not and should not produce individually identifiable results. Because the organization we were working for did not actually deliver workplace literacy programs, the newspaper hired a local literacy organization to deliver the program as based on our analysis and program recommendations. It began on a rocky road, with issues of attendee frustration and resentment, but the instructor built trust with the four workers and they progressed well enough to keep their jobs. So what were, for me, the key ethically related issues in this second scenario?

Along with the pressure of meeting our board member's request, we faced a high-risk situation. The rocky relationship between management and the union was all too evident, the threat of job loss imminent, the pressure for individualized test results intense, the mandatory nature of the program unchangeable, and the distinct possibility of my loss of professional reputation existed if we failed. Allow me some elaborations before ending.

Institutional Pressure. We faced real pressure to take on a workplace program under very unfavorable conditions. It is possible that had this prominent board member not asked for assistance, we would not have accepted a situation that presented so many possibilities for failure and contradictions with our professional principles. On the other hand, not to try to resolve the problems (as we defined them) and thus help these four workers keep their jobs would have made us very ethically challenged and psychologically stressed. On further reflection, this situation also raises the issue of promising too much through a workplace literacy program and thinking (without justification) that our intervention can address longstanding organizational issues.

I am not sure what we would do differently in any future scenario. Presented with a similar situation, but without the pressure-laden request of a board member, I may not say no; I would always want to see how far I could maneuver until the breaking point. However, if the HR manager had insisted on individual progress reports or the results of individual assessments, and with no intervention from a powerful board member, I absolutely would have said no.

Confidentiality. Belfiore (2002) reports that confidentiality of any kind of assessments or progress is high on good practice principles and that the confidentiality of individual assessments and learner progress is the most contentious area between employers and educators. Even though we indeed established that all results would be confidential, management agreed only with reluctance; they were denied the chance to fire workers.

I do not see *any* circumstances that would warrant making such risk-inducing personalized results available to management, or the union for that matter.

Testing. Testing of employees and the handover of individual test results are common requests from employers, in my experience. To guide my decision making, I ask: Is a test the assessment tool that will be most meaningful and useful in determining individual goals along with ways to build a program and learner confidence and participation? In almost every instance, my answer would be no. I would be ready with some alternatives, including an individual interview with potential program participants as to their needs and interests along with their own perceptions of where they want to focus, what they do well, and where they want to do better.

Management and Worker Cooperation. Although we consulted with both management and the union, they lacked any effective cooperation with each other. The union agreed to the program separately under certain conditions, but management and the union were not working in concert. In most workplace learning scenarios, this lack of cooperation would have been judged as a negative factor—indeed as a highly unusual context for establishing any learning program.

Joint Committee at a Plastics Factory: Not So Equal Participation

The third scenario focuses on the collaborative program planning process between workers and management. It presents a significant ethical issue that I still have not entirely resolved. For my colleagues and me, conducting ethnographic research in our respective workplaces cemented our understanding of the difficulty of collaborative planning mostly because of power differences between workers and management (Belfiore and others, 2004). We always knew that it was not easy to come to an understanding or common agreement on a policy and plan for a workplace literacy initiative because of such power differences. Belfiore (2002) notes, "The aim is to have people representing different perspectives working together with equal voices" (p. 24). She describes the committee role as planning, implementing, and monitoring workplace literacy initiatives. Committees are seen as a place where workers have a voice around their needs, all voices can be heard, and conflicting goals resolved. Though not a perfect decision mechanism, Belfiore notes that the committee at least is a forum where conflicts may be resolved.

Once upon a time, I worked with a joint committee of workers and management in a nonunionized plastics factory. We went through what I thought was a model joint planning process. The committee (with equal numbers of workers from different parts of the floor, and equal numbers of supervisors and managers) determined working principles and terms of reference, planned and conducted an organizational needs assessment, set priorities for programs, offered them, and planned the evaluation. When

New Directions for Adult and Continuing Education • DOI: 10.1002/ace

I interviewed the workers on the committee (as part of the evaluation process), I was surprised to find out that many had not been pleased with the committee process. They felt that decisions had been made without their input by the HR manager; that he had deliberately worked outside the committee process. They also believed that some of those decisions by the manager were brought to the committee only for rubber stamping.

Here I saw the results of how power differences in the workplace shape a collaborative planning process. It shows that equal participation is difficult, despite the democracy rhetoric, and that there may be a tendency to fall back on the usual procedures based on the usual power differentials operating in the workplace. To make matters worse, workers usually have not had the experience in, or training for, participation in such committees. But management personnel have. Some unions offer mentoring and training for union representatives on how to participate in these committees, but for a nonunionized workplace such training would be unusual. So, to adhere to my principle of inclusion of workers in decision making about their development, I must be more vigilant for seeing (1) covert signs of decisions already having been made outside the committee and (2) the threats and risks inherent in workers' participation in decision making.

To summarize, what does it mean for me to be an ethical literacy educator? My first thought is to always remember that the workplace is a complex, contested terrain where workers and managers have different and competing interests. As a workplace practitioner, I come back to the idea of staying grounded in my principles but adjusting my practice on the basis of new information and experience that makes sense but is still in line with these principles. I come back to the Spiral Model as a framework for deepening my ethical practice through an ongoing cycle of reflection on action and new ways of moving forward based on this reflection.

References

Arnold, R., Burke, B., James, C. Martin, D., and Thomas, B. *Educating for a Change.* Toronto: Doris Marshal Institute for Education and Action; Toronto: Between the Lines, 1991.

Belfiore, M. *Good Practice in Use.* Toronto: Ontario Literacy Coalition, 2002. Retrieved May 1, 2008, from http://www.on.literacy.ca/pubs/goodprac/cover.htm.

Belfiore, M., Defoe, T., Folinsbee, S., Jackson, N., and Hunter, J. *Reading Work: Literacies in the New Workplace.* Mahwah, N.J.: Erlbaum, 2004.

Connon-Unda, J. *Seeds for Change: A Curriculum Guide for Worker-Centred Literacy.* Ottawa: Canadian Labour Congress, 2001.

Folinsbee, S. "Looking Back, Looking Forward: A Conversation with Workplace Educators." Author, 2000. Retrieved May 1, 2008, from http://www.nald.ca/library/research/lookback/cover.htm.

Folinsbee, S., and Jurmo, P. *Collaborative Needs Assessment: A Handbook for Workplace Development Planners.* Toronto: ABC CANADA, 1994. Retrieved May 1, 2008, from http://www.nald.ca/FULLTEXT/abc/colnee/colnee.pdf.

Sork, T. J. "Ethical Issues in Program Planning." In R. G. Brockett (ed.), *Ethical Issues in Adult Education.* New York: Teachers College Press, 1988.

Steel, N., Johnston, W., Folinsbee, S., and Belfiore, M. "Towards a Framework of Good Practice." In M. Taylor (ed.), *Workplace Education: The Changing Landscape*. Toronto: Culture Concepts, 1997.

SUE FOLINSBEE is president of Tri En Communications in Toronto, Canada, and a long-time workplace learning practitioner and researcher.

New Directions for Adult and Continuing Education • DOI: 10.1002/ace

4

The author offers examples from his teaching about race and gender and discusses the ethical challenges faced and strategies employed to confront these challenges.

Just Democracy: Ethical Considerations in Teaching

Talmadge C. Guy

I am often caught in an ethical bind in my teaching. On the one hand, democratic participation strikes me as a worthy goal for my adult classrooms. Discussion, critical dialogue, and equitable participation values guide my teaching. On the other hand, classroom democratic practice is constrained by prejudiced patterns of behavior and attitudes.

Here I do not see myself as different from many colleagues: my classrooms are spaces and opportunities to create conversations among people that would probably not occur otherwise. But the reality is that the adult classroom is a microcosm, a particular instance within the larger social system, where we routinely find social hierarchy and inequality. Unlike in the broader context, the adult educator has considerable say over how social relationships are constructed; so I work at constructing dialogic, open-ended, and participatory environments in which all individuals, regardless of background or identity, can speak and be heard. But beyond this goal I have an agenda that is important in creating a democratic space within the wider social system.

Systems of unmerited privilege constantly nip at the edges of my practice. Dominant patterns of social interaction creep into the learning space I try to create. Whites want to speak authoritatively to and for other groups. White women, who predominate in most of my classes, want to set the tone for classroom discussion. International students of Asian descent are reluctant to speak openly, often as a result of the cultural norms that govern educational relationships; for them, silent observation may be the predominant

NEW DIRECTIONS FOR ADULT AND CONTINUING EDUCATION, no. 123, Fall 2009 © 2009 Wiley Periodicals, Inc.
Published online in Wiley InterScience (www.interscience.wiley.com) • DOI: 10.1002/ace.342

mode by which they engage the classroom. Black students may be cautious in expressing their views; many have learned to be guarded in predominantly white settings. Often, men, black or white, dominate the airtime, drowning out other voices. I struggle to navigate a course of action that is simultaneously inclusive of multiple views and multicultural and antiracist, antisexist.

My additional concern is to value, evaluate, and balance different points of view on a topic. They are often developed in terms of dominant and minority points of view. Here I am using *minority* in both of its meanings: minority as the view held by the smaller number of participants or even perhaps just by one, and minority as the representation of a marginalized discourse standing at odds with a dominant discourse. There have been times when my personal viewpoint accords with that of a single student. Sometimes it is precisely the viewpoint that I want to propose to the class in order to subject to critical analysis in relation to a dominant perspective. So when that individual student speaks her point of view and it goes unacknowledged or minimized, I decide to return to it and emphasize it—giving it credence by citing evidence or developing supporting logical argumentation.

Baptiste (2001) argues that democracy, as a model of adult education practice, is suitable only in essentially conciliatory situations. In such situations, stakeholders are potential allies, forming a community in which disagreements are relatively easily and peacefully resolved. However, when teaching focuses on difficult issues of race and racism difference, honest dialogue may often become conflict not easily resolved. To strive for inclusion, racial justice, and multiculturalism entails the undoing of overt and covert privilege and white supremacy in the classroom—covert because it almost never happens anymore that adult learners are overt about their bias or prejudice against persons of color. Instead racism assumes a colorblind mask and goes underground, with the consequence that it is much subtler and more challenging to surface.

Some examples

My classes at the University of Georgia typically address issues of race, class, and gender (RCG). Despite considerable experience here, I am frequently on edge in my classes because I realize how difficult these topics are for many graduate students. I also know that some do not want to engage in discussion about diversity and will go to great lengths to avoid them. In the examples here, I point to sources of conflict and I foreground the challenges to balance my obligation to promote learning with my sense of justice, fairness, and inclusion.

Black Equals Less Than. In several of my classes I introduce readings and discussion on RCG issues. In a discussion of race, difference, and deficiency, Joyce (a pseudonym), an African American woman in my class, presented an experience involving her son's schooling. The class already had talked about how ethnic or racial difference from the white norm is often construed as deficiency in education. Several students offered their partially theoretical analyses, but Joyce spoke from her own experience as an African American mother of two now-grown sons (all information that could potentially identify students from any quotations has been changed to protect identities):

> I was also struck by the statement that diversity is often linked with deficiency. But even more so by the statements that led up to it, which describe a "language of deficiency" . . . sometimes portrayed as a lack of motivation, self-esteem, etc. This idea of deficiency becomes so strongly tied with race so that anytime you're speaking of black students, even adult students, deficiency is assumed. . . . Throughout my sons' elementary, middle, and high school years, I was constantly battling the educators about what I considered "labeling" of my sons. It happened more with my eldest son, but more often than not we had to have major "sit-down" meetings with my son's teachers to get them on the same page with us. Henry is very intelligent, but you had to make an effort to reach him. He was into rap music in its early stages, and he thought differently than other kids. He was an African American kid whose teachers were usually white. I had one teacher tell me that when he first saw him, he thought, "There was a kid who never should have been accepted into this (model) school!" I believe they just couldn't relate to him. As it turns out, my son is finishing a [graduate] program . . . this semester. There was never anything "wrong" with him.

The reaction to this story was swift and empathic. Some students who struggled with the idea that difference was often seen as deficiency rushed to empathize with Joyce and bemoan her terrible experiences. Some in the class wondered if her story was an aberrant situation. Emboldened by Joyce's narrative, several other students also spoke about the challenges they face as parents in trying to support their children against indifferent or biased teachers. Joyce's narrative is a counter story (Solórzano & Yosso, 2002) that provides factual evidence about her experience; her story transforms the classroom into a place where knowledge is shared about the subtle but ever-present ways in which oppression—in this case, racial—operates.

This example illustrates what is possible in a classroom that is diverse and in which adults feel free to express their viewpoints. There was little need for me to nudge or direct the classroom conversation. As I listened to Joyce's story, I was pleased that it made precisely the point, ever so eloquently, that I wanted the class to appreciate and internalize. The fact that it was a story from Joyce's personal experience made it real and impactful for all of us. Little action was needed, other than allowing the discussion to ensue without my interference (except for filling in points or identifying related research). This example shows how class discussions about race, class, or gender may happen to open up learning and validate the experience of those

on the margins. However, I also experience class sessions that are less conciliatory and more resistant to divergent views.

Reverse Discrimination and White Privilege. Class interactions that
verge on serious conflict pose real challenges for me. Though infrequent,
they happen often enough that I continually ponder strategies to address
classroom conflicts. In this particular class (with more than twenty students,
mostly white and mostly female), almost everyone lived and worked in different parts of Georgia—in educational institutions, in service agencies, in
the corporate sector, and in nonprofit organizations. In one class, we were
discussing racial differences and white privilege. I had asked students to discuss the concept of privilege. Objecting to the notion of white privilege,
David, a white male student, replied this way:

> There are black magazines, *Black Enterprises, Black Men, Black Issues, Black
> Beat,* and the list goes on and on. There are hundreds of black organizations.
> The National Black Business Trade Association, the National Black Police
> Association, the National Black Media Coalition, 1,000 Black Men, etc., etc.
> The black-only contests: Black Miss America, Black Athlete of the Year, and
> several more. What do you think would happen if there was a White Miss
> America contest? or a *White Enterprises* magazine? or a whites-only club? Al
> Sharpton would be all over that!! There is absolutely NO WAY that any of
> those things would ever happen.
>
> I bring up this point because I think that these black only things are harm-
> ful to race relations. It's completely acceptable and alright for black people to
> have all of these exclusively black things, but whites would be seen as bigots
> and racists if they did. Now me—I wouldn't be a member of a whites-only fra-
> ternity. I wouldn't be interested in a whites-only magazine. I wouldn't even
> consider joining a whites-only country club. That's not my point. I realize
> how oppressed blacks have been in this country for so many years, but does
> it really help to have what I view as reverse racism? I'm just curious what oth-
> ers think about this?

Yvonne, who was white, made it a point to agree with David and support him in his "courage" to state his views honestly. She asserted: "I think
we all share your same view, but just don't know quite how to say it." Two
African American students emailed me about their discomfort over David's
statement. I realized, from past experience and from the literature, that as a
black male my views could be seen as biased, reflecting a particular agenda,
and therefore lacking legitimacy. While I considered how to proceed,
Jeanette responded:

> I don't mean to pick on David. . . . I just want to illuminate the idea that there
> are more complaints about black television, black magazines, etc. . . . and lit-
> tle is said about other groups who express their right to unite and embrace
> that which brings them together as a common people. It doesn't mean that

New Directions for Adult and Continuing Education • DOI: 10.1002/ace

they ONLY want to associate with that one group. And in regards to the suggestion that if white people had only white magazines, white television, white clubs, etc. . . . well, again I may offend some when I state that we already have that. They aren't LABELLED white only. . . . And why do we have to use words like "reverse discrimination"? And . . . it is also my opinion that the idea that discrimination can be reversed is a farce. . . . I find that idea as ridiculous as assuming everyone is white unless otherwise stated. Why BEGIN with white?

Elaine added that white was the norm for many organizations—"like the DAR [Daughters of the American Revolution], which I belong to. . . . It is almost impossible for a Black person to prove they are descendants of a Revolutionary War solder, or someone who assisted the colonists in their fight for independence." Nevertheless, David persisted: "I think that if there was an attempt to have a White Miss America pageant all hell would break loose. I just feel that both are wrong."

As David was talking, I thought simply to factually correct David's view of black organizations. Jeanette's reply was right on point—exactly what I thought should be said. But what happens often—and certainly did in this case—was that her reply was ignored. It appeared to make no difference at all in David's thinking. He chose not to address what she said. To the contrary, she addressed his argument, point by point. Most American organizations, institutions, and practices were, by default, white. I worried that David, and other students who lurked in silent agreement, would retreat into quiet resistance. I am quite aware that some whites take such action as a part of their privilege—to ignore, minimize, or otherwise push to the margins—any point of view that decenters whiteness. This dismissal becomes a teachable moment, but I also realize that white students often view, as reverse discrimination, race discussions that decenter whiteness. (I hasten to add here that even though these examples are grounded in issues of racial privilege and marginalization, similar situations also arise with respect to gender and class.)

Classroom discussions that embody racial conflict often present value conflicts that must be navigated very carefully. Ethical dilemmas span a range of situations, but I have found that it is counterproductive to think in terms of abstract, ethical principles applicable to any moral challenge. In these examples, how I exert my professorial authority can shape in a significant way any learning that takes place. I sometimes wonder how a white professor would handle similar proceedings. Teacher positionality can affect how learners respond to and interpret teacher explanations on race, class, or gender. Because most of the students in my classes are white, I am very cognizant of my own positionality and ponder how to balance what I say and how I say it. On the other hand, I also understand that some students simply are not open to particular viewpoints, despite my giving research-based and theoretically sound resources.

Ethical Issues

In *Teaching to Transgress,* bell hooks (1994) offers a view of teaching that I still try to incorporate into my classrooms. Her idea of engaged pedagogy means "that teachers must be actively involved and committed to a process of self-actualization that promotes their own well-being if they are to teach in a manner that empowers students" (p. 15). Employing democratic practices when dealing with tough RCG issues may set up conditions in which teachers fail to attend to their own well-being. The classroom environment and its interactions may suffer when students challenge or resist teachers committed to a view of social justice. Teachers may engage in self-doubt or become demoralized and stressed. Under such circumstances, teachers may sometimes resort to undemocratic practices in the name of pursuing their view of ethically just practice (Freedman, 2007).

An unfettered ethical commitment to democratic educational practice worries me for at least three reasons. Democracy is commonly taken to mean majority rule. The premise that everyone has an equal opportunity to express his or her point of view is rarely realized, even under the most favorable conditions. The win-lose aspect implied in democratic practice cuts against the aim of creating a democratic community in which there is a sharing of experience and a co-construction of knowledge. One of the first challenges I face in a classroom is to set aside the common idea that the viewpoint that is most widely held is the preferred one. (In the public domain, this happens every four years during the presidential election cycle: the point of view most widely held typically wins—the 2000 presidential election notwithstanding.) Widely held opinions may be taken as true but in fact are often completely wrong. When class participants hold a majoritarian (Solórzano & Yosso, 2002) point of view, the teacher is placed in the position of adjudicating the preferred view. Discussions of race, class, or gender then are rarely deliberated in purely objective or dispassionate ways. When the majority position is associated with a particular racial, ethnic, gender positionality (white, male, for example), the choices that teachers make become critical for creating a learning environment seen by participants as both democratic and liberatory.

For an African American male who teaches predominantly white women graduate students, I find such challenges significant. Questions constantly arise: Does my male privilege work at odds with my racial identity? In addressing problems of racial inequality, where should I draw the line between my teacher's authority and my commitment to helping learners see tough issues in new and liberating ways? Whose experience should guide the curriculum? I confess that it can be tempting at times to let a majoritarian viewpoint "sit there," as it were, even if I realize that it needs to be challenged. I often find myself carefully calculating when and how to

New Directions for Adult and Continuing Education • DOI: 10.1002/ace

challenge majoritarian perspectives on race, class, or gender. Contrary to hooks's admonition to teachers, I feel quite exhausted when I leave class and at times discouraged about my decision making.

The utopian dimension within the American democratic tradition conceals how power is exercised and inequality produced and reproduced. Democratic process that gives symbolic voice only to the marginalized is not an adequate solution to development of democratic community or to a sense of fairness or justice. The problem with the utopian view is that American democracy becomes more expansive and just only after a struggle by those who were initially marginalized in the political process. Inclusion of women, African Americans, and Japanese Americans (among others) in the political process came as a result of challenging dominant power structures and traditional understandings of democracy. Power yields nothing except with a struggle. Teachers who attempt to create classrooms where everyone feels "safe" pursue a dubious goal, in my opinion. I think rather of creating RCG classrooms where participants understand that it is all right—indeed expected—to be challenged and to feel uncomfortable.

Brookfield (2005) summarizes democratic practice by saying: "good discussion, and therefore good democratic process, depends on everyone contributing, on everyone having the fullest possible knowledge of different perspectives" (pp. 265–266). When democracy is understood as a right accorded to those of a particular status—say, citizen—who then bear responsibility for exercising that right, then the lack of participation is seen simply as forgoing one's rights. As an act of withdrawal from the political process, democracy is unaffected because it depends on the choice to actively participate by citizens. In the classroom, the choice not to participate—in effect, to not engage in critical dialogue—works against a liberatory process (Brookfield and Preskill, 2005). I recall numerous occasions when students have sat silently in response to a critical point I or someone else makes in the class about race. Although not all silence is resistance, it often feels that way when teaching issues of race. This result raises several questions. How much should I respect the right of students to not engage in discussion? Am I justified in interpreting silence as resistance and the exercise of unmerited privilege? What is my responsibility to interrupt what I take as oppressive discourse of behavior? Are some actions unethical in interrupting oppression? In other words, do the ends necessarily justify the means in the pursuit of justice?

These ethical challenges grow out of a view of democratic practice that follows in the tradition of Dewey and Lindeman, who saw adult education as contributing to democratic living and to the development of community, as opposed to the exercise of individual rights. My reading of Lindeman is that the moral value "freedom" really should be understood as "freedom with," which embodies the idea that in the adult classroom we are not entitled to retreat into our own personally held point of view because we then undermine the growth and development of the group. As Lindeman (1926) points out, freedom can never be completely devoid of any social interaction. I like this reading of Lindeman because I see how easy it is for racial dialogue to regress into talking only to those who share an opinion. In my classroom, the idea of silence on topics of racial dialogue means that we exercise freedom as "freedom from."

Another aspect of majoritarian silence and resistance is that the narratives of women and persons of color often become minimized or ignored. I have talked with many African American students (and other racial or ethnic minority students as well) who, for various reasons, are reluctant to share their personal experiences with racism or sexism in the classroom. Perhaps because of my own personal history, I feel a connection to these students, and I see myself as having a responsibility for creating a safe space for them to tell their stories. I have come to terms with the idea that I can be perceived as showing favoritism—as one student wrote on the end of course evaluation, "advancing [my] personal agenda."

Working My Way Through Ethical Challenges

Let me return to the example of reverse discrimination and white privilege. Online discussions of RCG tend to be more open, where students feel more empowered to say what they really think and feel. I appreciated David for offering his opinion, but what is always a touchy issue is how to manage the discussion—which has, on occasion, turned ugly. As soon as I read David's comment, I began to think how I should reply. One of the challenges of teaching RCG online is that I cannot read body language or affect. I was therefore concerned about writing something that would be seen as off-putting. David had a right to express his opinion, but I wanted to show that what he said was just that, and a not well-informed one. Saying to someone "you are wrong" can be off-putting, so I tried to think of tactful but forceful language that would cause him to consider alternative explanations to the racial phenomena under focus. My concern also was to elicit a response, rather than to shut him down. The democratic classroom, at least how I think about it, should encourage multiple viewpoints in the interest of promoting a critical examination of all viewpoints. In David's case, Jeanette's message did exactly that, so I sent a private message to Jeanette approving of her comment so she would be encouraged to continue to speak out. Why? Her comment stated what I would have said, and I wanted to avoid her feeling unsupported. David's last reply— simply a restatement of his original position—led me to think that he was shutting down. I encouraged him to explain his viewpoint, especially in light of the readings we were discussing, and asked him to consider why there continue to be significant structural inequalities along racial lines. He replied:

New Directions for Adult and Continuing Education • DOI: 10.1002/ace

It is now illegal to discriminate in the United States based on race/color and there are more lawyers per capita in the U.S. than any nation on earth. If there is discrimination going on (and I'm sure there is in many different ways), a juicy lawsuit or hefty settlement is just one legal proceeding away. There are programs and institutions to specifically help the black community (Rainbow Coalition, NAACP, Negro College Fund, affirmative action, etc.). Maybe we need more community involvement; more education about the services available? So I don't know why there is inequity, but it seemed to me that Bonilla-Silva [a class reading] discounts any reason other than white racism against blacks.

How far should I carry my teacher's authority in developing a reply? I could certainly take the position that he was a student and should read what I ask. On the other hand, this was exactly the kind of approach that verges on "banking education," which would lead to his further resistance. I struggled with how to keep a pedagogically healthy communication going with him.

In this narrative, I also recall discussions with other colleagues of color who struggle with similar issues. I often hear that "you can only do so much" and that "you can't expect to successfully fight white privilege, especially at a predominantly white institution like the University of Georgia." But I refuse to give up the idea that I am a teacher with something to teach; nor do I wish to give up the idea that cross-race dialogues can produce democratic communities of learning in which we affirm and honor multiple points of view while moving toward a sense of socially just and equitable relationships. Ethically I felt justified in supporting and prompting Jeanette's point of view. I could easily have left the discussion there, but I need to work out ways of reaching across racial boundaries to challenge white supremacy and privilege—even at the risk of alienating those very people I am trying to reach. I try to strike a balance between my commitment to an ethic of racial justice and inclusion while using ethical strategies of inclusion, pluralism, and dialogue. I am also forced to strike a balance between my own positionality as an African American male and my privilege, authority, and power as a male professor. There is no easy answer to either of these ethical challenges.

Summary

Cornel West's statement "Democracy is an indeterminate solution to an insoluble problem" (1993) is an apt way to conclude. Ethical decision making in democratic adult classroom must be understood as complex, prone to miscalculation, and ultimately achieving only partial answers to the problems of teaching about race, class, or gender (Usher, Bryant, and Johnston, 1997). The ethical principles of pluralism, inclusion, fairness, and justice turn out to be ideals to which we strive (Baptiste, 2001), not determinate paths we follow. I ask you to think more about this profoundly difficult issue: Is democratic practice ever fully realizable in a society where structured inequality is constitutive of our social system? Is democracy ever fully realizable in the adult classroom where race, class, and gender issues form the basic subject matter? What can I do to achieve ethically just democratic practice in my work?

References

Baptiste, I. "Exploring the Limits of Participatory Democracy: Prudent and Decisive Use of Authority in Adult Education." In D. Ntiri (ed.), *Politicization and Democratization of Adult Education: Models for Adult and Lifelong Learning* (Vol. 3). Detroit: Wayne State University Press, 2001.

Brookfield, S. *The Power of Critical Theory: Liberating Adult Learning and Teaching.* San Francisco: Jossey-Bass, 2005.

Brookfield, S., and Preskill, S. *Discussion as a Way of Teaching: Tools and Techniques for Democratic Classrooms* (2nd ed.). San Francisco: Jossey-Bass, 2005.

Freedman, E. B. "Is Teaching for Social Justice Undemocratic?" *Harvard Educational Review,* 77, 2007.

hooks, b. *Teaching to Transgress: Education as the Practice of Freedom.* New York: Routledge, 1994.

Lindeman, E. C. *The Meaning of Adult Education.* New York, New Republic, 1926.

Solórzano, D. G., & Yosso, T. J. "Critical Race Methodology: Counter-Story Telling as an Analytical Framework for Education." *Qualitative Inquiry,* 2002, *8,* 23–44.

Usher, R., Bryant, I., and Johnston, R. *Adult Education and the Postmodern Challenge: Learning Beyond the Limits.* New York: Routledge, 1997.

West, C. *Race Matters.* Boston: Beacon Press, 1993.

TALMADGE C. GUY *is associate professor of lifelong education, administration, and policy and teaches in the adult education program at the University of Georgia in Athens, Georgia.*

5

This chapter examines practical problems encountered in mentoring adult learners in higher education through stories of ethical dilemmas.

Ethical Issues in Mentoring Adults in Higher Education

Catherine A. Hansman

How does an adult educator unpack ethical issues within mentoring contexts, especially when those issues nest in interpersonal relationships? In my experience of mentoring adults to complete significant academic tasks, a variety of uncomfortable situations may arise, slowly, but inexorably—for example, between the mentor's self-protection needs and the protégé's right to appropriate guidance, or between my wanting a courteous and calm academic relationship and my realization that the students needed to hear frank and potentially discomforting news about their standard of work. Such conflicts have caused me to reflect about the challenges in the interactions between a mentor and a protégé. So before going into more detail about actual scenarios, I outline key points about the goals and processes of mentoring to set the scene.

Informal learning "refers to the experiences of everyday living from which we learn something" (Merriam, Caffarella, and Baumgartner, 2007, p. 24). For adults, many informal learning experiences involve working with someone else, such as a mentor, who may engage them in learning activities to help promote growth and development. The mentors "have been unquestioningly and uncritically accepted as fundamental to foster learning in the workplace, advance careers, help new employees learn workplace culture, and provide developmental and psychological support" (Hansman, 2002a, p. 39). Mentors can play key roles in their protégés' personal and professional development. However, the roles in which both mentors and protégés engage are mitigated by how those involved describe

NEW DIRECTIONS FOR ADULT AND CONTINUING EDUCATION, no. 123, Fall 2009 © 2009 Wiley Periodicals, Inc.
Published online in Wiley InterScience (www.interscience.wiley.com) • DOI: 10.1002/ace.343

mentoring relationships and define the roles of mentors and protégés. For instance, Daloz (1986) characterizes mentors as guides and interpreters of landscapes for protégés, so it would seem that mentors help protégés understand and deal effectively with their life contexts. Caffarella's ideas (1993) of mentoring relationships focus on "intense caring relationships" (p. 28) in which persons with more experience mentor less experienced colleagues to promote personal and professional growth, and they point to the significant roles mentors can play in the lives of their protégés.

Mentoring relationships can take many forms, from formal agreements or programs to informal and mutually agreed relationships. Formal mentoring programs "embody professional and workplace themes and are generally organized and sponsored by workplaces or professional organizations" (Hansman, 2003, p. 101). Informal mentoring relationships are "dependent on the relationship developed between mentor and protégé . . . mentors and protégés choose each other usually based on similar interests or attraction" (Hansman, 2000, p. 494).

Universities are the sites for many types of mentoring relationships, both formal and informal. Formal relationships can include faculty members advising and chairing doctoral dissertations, thesis, or other student projects, while an example of informal mentoring relationships might be senior faculty mentoring junior faculty members or students to assist them in reaching their career, and possibly personal, goals. I have been fortunate, over several careers, to have had many mentors who reflected the roles described by Caffarella and Daloz in both formal, arranged mentoring relationships and informal ones. While a doctoral student, for example, many mentors guided me across the rocky terrain to researching and writing my dissertation and then, when I was a junior faculty member, guided me along the path to tenure and promotion.

Now, in my own professorial work with master's and doctoral students, I borrow from others' ideas of mentors and think of myself as an advisor, sponsor, and at times facilitator of change with my student protégés. As evident in the opening question of this chapter, I often ponder my current role as a mentor and my past protégé role, knowing that because of the intense personal interactions between mentors and protégés, ethical issues can be sources of anxiety for both. Mentors, by their institutional or societal roles, have power that can help or harm their protégés (Hansman, 2000, 2002a, 2002b, 2003, 2005). Along with power issues in mentoring relationships are the considerations of how race, class, and gender may affect the availability of mentors to some protégés (Hansman, 2002a; Johnson-Bailey and Cervero, 2002), and how mentors may have the power to challenge negative "isms" (racism, sexism, classism, ageism) that favor some over others. Through cross-mentoring situations where mentors from dominant cultures may mentor members of minority groups, mentors can challenge the *status quo* and provide support to protégés.

New Directions for Adult and Continuing Education • DOI: 10.1002/ace

Each incident described in this chapter illustrates the power that mentors possess and the ethical challenges of using this power to help or hurt protégés. Each example addresses an aspect of such power: the power to remove oneself as a mentor, the power to challenge and inspire, the power to not communicate reasons for actions, and the power to protect protégés. After my reflections on the ethical dynamics and challenges I uncover in each situation, my own set of key ethical mentoring principles concludes the chapter.

Helping Hillary: Resistance and Letting Go

Hillary was a thirtysomething white woman who was researching and writing her dissertation. She asked me to cochair and mentor her through the process. She had been a student in my class for several years. She was very affable, and we became friends outside of the mentor-protégé relationship, attending some social events together. I was still new on campus, a junior faculty member, and I had not yet achieved tenure, so I welcomed opportunities to make friends and explore the community. At this point I thought of her as a friend, and I looked forward to mentoring her and working with her through the dissertation process.

I was cochair, not chair, of her dissertation because her topic (math education) and methodology (quantitative) were not my specialty areas. At this point, when I realized that her research interests and mine were not compatible, and that I probably did not have the expertise she needed, I should have removed myself from her committee. But her topic did include some aspects of adult education (developmental studies, second chance adult students), and because I had previously taught English in developmental studies at another university, I knew the research regarding developmental studies. I had been her teacher in the past and she felt comfortable with me, so I agreed to cochair her dissertation with James, an older man from the education faculty who was more familiar than I with the math focus of her topic.

As we moved closer to her proposal hearing, I became troubled. It was clear that she had poor writing skills that translated into a difficult-to-read proposal. James and I worked with her to help improve her writing. At her proposal hearing, the other members of her committee and I had suggestions for reframing her ideas. During the hearing, Hillary seemed to agree with the need to make the proposed changes. We also suggested that she use the campus writing center; she agreed to visit the center. After the hearing, my friendship with Hillary seemed to come to an end, which I felt was appropriate because we had moved into a different, more professional mentoring relationship.

When we next heard from Hillary several months later, she had written all five chapters of her dissertation. She brought them to James and me

New Directions for Adult and Continuing Education • DOI: 10.1002/ace

for our review, comments, and suggestions. As I read her chapters, my concerns rose: her writing was not very clear and thus her dissertation was difficult to understand, she had not made the changes agreed on in her proposal hearing, and she made statements regarding returning adult learners that I found offensive (they were lazy, poor, not willing to work) and at times somewhat racist. She had no data with which to support such statements, but nevertheless there they were.

I challenged her on her offensive statements, but she argued with me about keeping them in her study. She agreed to remove them from her dissertation only when I told her that I could no longer cochair her dissertation. However, after she removed these statements it became clear from things she said and did that she viewed me as a hindrance to her finishing her dissertation. We eventually enlisted the aid of a third party, a mutual friend, John, to "mediate" our meetings. Through John's intervention, with James's help and my oversight, Hillary eventually wrote a passable doctoral dissertation and graduated.

Hillary is now serving as an instructor and lecturer. I do not have any communication with her, and I can only assume that she feels I made her process toward earning her dissertation extremely difficult and does not think of my actions as helpful to her. Our formal mentoring relationship ended when she finished her dissertation.

Reflection. The mentoring of Hillary is a clear example of the power that mentors hold and can choose to judiciously use to force changes that may be unwanted and felt or experienced as unhelpful by the protégé. As I reflect on this incident, I feel justified in my threatening to quit as her mentor because it was not an idle threat: I really would have removed myself from the committee if she had not made the required changes to her dissertation. However, I believe my actions resulted in her writing a better dissertation. I had hoped, though, that through challenging her offensive statements and biased thinking I might have sparked some level of transformation in her views of returning adult students and in her ability to produce a possibly publishable piece of research (especially because she aimed for a full-time faculty position). However, given the conditions I faced, I wonder what I could have done differently to be more supportive as a mentor while at the same time challenging her to a higher level of reflection, data analysis, and writing. Admittedly, my own inexperience then as a mentor to doctoral students hindered my thinking and actions; I needed a mentor myself, and I should have asked for help from a more senior faculty member. But at the time, as an untenured faculty member, I did not want to seem helpless, and I had my own tenure concerns. So I made the best decisions possible at the time. I should have stepped away from Hillary's committee when I first realized that her topic was an area about which I was not an expert. But because of the limited number of faculty members willing to work with doctoral students, I also felt obligated to serve on her committee. Had I not been on her committee and we maintained a friendship, then perhaps as a friend I might have been better able to challenge her thinking.

In this case, my power as a mentor and my inexperience in working with doctoral students both helped and hurt the protégé. It certainly bruised my feelings in the process, although I learned many things about mentoring students. First, mentors may be friendly with their protégés, but friendships between mentors and protégés are tricky and have the potential to hurt both parties involved. Second, mentors themselves need their own mentors at times, and they should consider finding and asking for help in challenging situations.

Darla's Dissertation Dilemma: Mentoring to Challenge and Inspire

Darla, a middle-aged African American doctoral student, is currently my student advisee and protégé. After completing all her doctoral classes and passing her comprehensive examinations, she has been working with me to craft her dissertation proposal. Besides engaging in her doctoral degree, Darla also works full-time in a demanding job. Because of her strong performance on the job, she was recently promoted to a position that requires even more from her in terms of energy and dedication. In addition, Darla has a challenging personal life; she lives with and provides assistance to an elderly relative and also gives frequent help to other members of her extended family. In short, she faces many blocks to finishing her dissertation—the kinds of barriers found in the adult education literature (Darkenwald and Valentine, 1985; Sissel, Hansman, and Kasworm, 2002; Merriam, Caffarella and Baumgartner, 2007). Consequently, she places a low priority on writing her dissertation proposal.

When I first started working with Darla as her dissertation advisor and faculty mentor, she and I often discussed her family situation, her work responsibilities, and her progress (or lack thereof) in honing her dissertation topic and writing her proposal. I was (and still am) very sympathetic to all the conflicting commitments her personal obligations and career place on her. However, as semesters passed without a real focus emerging for her dissertation, or even the beginnings of her proposal, I began to realize that my role as sympathetic and caring mentor needed to change. Our conversations, instead of focusing on her dissertation, research purpose, and research questions, were all too frequently about her barriers and obstacles to researching and writing.

I become conscious that all the sympathy and understanding in the world were not going to move Darla to write her dissertation proposal. I questioned my actions as an understanding mentor and realized that I was perhaps not acting in a truly ethical manner for her to achieve her goal of completing her doctoral degree. My work with her, though giving sympathy and understanding, was not what she needed. I knew that there were many factors about which I had no control, such as her family and work situations, but at least I could change my interactions with her to challenge her into the needed focus on research and writing.

Granted, this realization was perhaps too long in coming to me; I wish I had done something earlier to facilitate her research and writing. But after much reflection, I resolved to interact with Darla differently in our next meetings. I now knew that in order to assist her, I had to hear her "true" goals. In short, I needed to know if she wanted my support to finish her dissertation and graduate. Or were our meetings only a way for her to unload her problems to a sympathetic ear? Instead of spending most of our time together discussing her litany of problems and responsibilities, I resolved to listen to her problems for a short period of time, then interrupt, and ask her some questions regarding her research and her goals on finishing her dissertation.

I put this plan into action during my next meeting with her, and the changes I made seemed to help us both engage in honest dialogue about her goals and her dissertation. As a result, I discovered that one of her aspirations after completing the degree is to retire and become a consultant. Once she articulated this goal, we discussed her ideas for research in more depth than was possible in our past conversations, including how her research might help her achieve these future goals. We also formulated a meeting schedule and a work plan with short-term writing and research goals for each meeting. Darla now makes progress in her research and writing, and our interactions include more intellectual discourse than was possible before this frank discussion.

Reflection. This case may seem to be a simple problem with a straightforward solution, but it is more complex than it appears. Because I had struggled to complete my own dissertation and, like Darla, also had competing personal and work problems, I was overly sympathetic to the issues that Darla was encountering. But to be a caring and helpful mentor, I had to leave behind my feelings about my own history and review Darla and her work in order to use my power as a mentor to challenge her to work beyond her problems.

Many mentors face the ethical concern I encountered here: how to support protégés in a caring manner while simultaneously challenging them to succeed. If I had continued to supply unlimited sympathy but did not challenge Darla or offer her strong leadership, I would have violated my values and ethical principles concerning mentoring students. For me, the ethic of care, "fundamentally concerned with how human beings meet and treat each other" (Noddings, 1993, p. 45), is an essential element in healthy mentoring relationships. Mentors need to understand their protégés' actual goals by asking protégés directly to articulate them. Mentors and protégés also should clearly communicate their expectations of each other.

Equivocal Endings: When Mentoring Is Over. Many mentoring relationships are informal and formed on the basis of mutual interests or goals, which may change over time, causing relationships to end, at times unexpectedly. Relationships may end for a variety of reasons; for example, conflict between mentor and protégé, changes in work or school situations, or loss of interest in maintaining the relationship by either or both the mentor or protégé. However, in my view, the worst endings are when a mentor "quits" mentoring and leaves the relationship but does not communicate to the protégé that she or he is ending the relationship.

As graduate student and later junior faculty in my first teaching position, I was a protégé in a couple of mentoring relationships (and experienced losing a mentor this way). In both cases, my mentors were senior faculty members, white males who were successful in their fields. They both showed initial interest in my work and were helpful in facilitating my growth as a future faculty member and in guiding me through understanding academe. With their help, I was able to present and publish papers, essential tasks for junior faculty members who are seeking tenure. Through their excellent coaching, I learned principles regarding teaching adults and classroom strategies that framed my instructional practice and improved my teaching.

I had good relationships with both of these mentors, or so I thought. But gradually, as time went on, I noticed that they seemed to disappear from my life. I was busy teaching, researching, and offering service, as well as raising my family as a single parent, so at first I did not notice that my emails, phone calls, and other communications to my mentors were not returned. As time went on, however, it became clear to me that I was not a part of their professional lives anymore. They had clearly ended their roles as my mentors, but for whatever reason they did not communicate this to me, nor give me reasons for ending our relationships.

As I realized that these men were no longer willing to support me as mentors, I was disappointed and upset. I did not, and still do not, know exactly why the relationships ended, so I can only speculate about the endings and the issues that may have precipitated them. Several questions that I have asked myself about these relationships are still unanswered: Did I not live up to their expectations? Were they angry that I was late getting back to them about research and writing projects? Did they give up on me achieving my goals? Did they think I no longer needed to be mentored? Was cross mentoring (males mentoring females or vice versa) an issue that factored into ending the relationships? Or did they simply become too busy to mentor me? Finally, because we were at different universities and communities, were space and distance a problem in maintaining our relationships? Instead of honestly addressing each situation, I chose to accept their decisions and let the relationships end. But because I did not discuss it with them, the questions I have listed still haunt me.

Reflection.   Mentoring, because it involves interpersonal relationships, can cause unexpected pain to protégés (and to mentors) when it ends, and unacknowledged endings are particularly difficult. Protégés may forever wonder why the mentoring relationship ended, particularly if mentors do not communicate with them why they are ending it. Protégés may blame themselves, looking for real or imagined issues, when in fact mentors may end relationships for many other reasons than problems with the protégé, such as lack of time to invest in the relationship. If mentors are encountering issues with protégés, however, and the problems can be addressed by the protégés (such as not following through on projects), then mentors should help their protégés understand that these issues are hurting their credibility in the relationship. If mentors truly wish to help their protégés, honest assessment in a nonpunitive fashion is essential to support their protégés.

As I look back on my actions here, I wish the "more experienced" me could tell the "neophyte" me to gather courage and ask my mentors why they no longer were willing to work with me. At the time, though, I was new to academe and did not want to challenge my mentors. I also accepted that some of my actions had probably contributed to the end of these relationships; I had not followed through on several things in a timely manner with these mentors. I recognized the power my mentors had, and because they were respected members of their fields I did not feel empowered to question their decisions related to mentoring me. Clearly I chose the path of least resistance in these relationships. Open communication and acknowledgment from my mentors regarding why they were ending the relationships were missing. By not questioning them, I am forever clueless as to exactly why these relationships ended.

Challenging to Protect: Mentors as Defenders

As a faculty member, I have many colleagues who are wonderful mentors and advisors to their graduate students. However, I also have some colleagues who have seem to have very negative views of their students. They engage in "trash talk" about students—during both private and public meetings, they enter into negative discussions concerning our graduate students, adult learners to whom we owe ethical behavior because they are our advisees and protégés.

Some of the negative collegial comments about students are justified (not turning in assignments, not showing up for class, being tardy for appointments). Other comments, however, point toward their generally negative view of all students, but particularly those adult learners who may have intrinsic and extrinsic issues, conflicting work and family tensions, and time and funding problems, all of which hinder their performance and motivation (Merriam, Caffarella, and Baumgartner, 2007; Sissel, Hansman, and Kasworm, 2002).

In the past, I listened to overly critical comments by colleagues about students and usually offered little challenge to their negative statements. After all, these were people with whom I worked, sat with in meetings, and assisted in planning programs. But for several years now I have become aware of how my avoidance of challenging my negative colleagues was not helping my protégés, as well as probably harming the protégés of the colleagues making pessimistic comments. In addition, my silence could be construed as acquiescence to their views, and further, it was preventing me from being the supportive mentor I hoped to be with my own students.

So I began to confront my colleagues when they made critical statements about students without real justifications for these statements. I also began to tackle them when they seemed to lump all adult students into one generic poor-performing group. At first, because I do not like confrontations, these actions felt quite uncomfortable. As I grew stronger in my beliefs concerning their cynical views and the negative energy they produced, I began to understand that challenging them was part of the power I hold as a mentor to student protégés. This realization helped me to be a better advocate and protector of my students' interests. I hope it helps my negative colleagues think differently about the students with whom they work. This dilemma is ongoing, and I still struggle with the best way to deal with it.

Reflection. The work of faculty members with their students as mentors and protégés is complex. Nevertheless, this situation illustrates several ethical issues involving mentoring students and protégés. First, in discussing their students and protégés in a negative fashion with other faculty members, mentors are breaking and violating the confidentiality they share with their protégés. Further, because of such negative assessments and public discussion of their students and protégés, they may deter other faculty members from working with their protégés in the future, which then may create problems for individual students. Mentors must use their power to protect their protégés, so I hope I am walking my talk and using this power to protect and support my protégés and other students.

Final Thoughts: Mentoring Maxims

I claim no expertise as a mentor, yet I have learned much from my work with protégés as well as being a protégé myself. What is essential is a healthy relationship between the mentor and protégé. Further, ethical considerations must remain forefront in mentors' minds. So here are my three key maxims.

Do No Harm. These words, widely yet erroneously attributed to the Hippocratic Oath, are very appropriate for mentors. But it is a difficult principle to follow, especially when well-intentioned frank comments about the quality of a student's work may, unjustifiably, be taken as an intrusion into a private world or as an outright insult to intelligence. Doing no harm to, or protecting, a protégé may mean doing some perceived harm to someone else, as in publicly challenging insensitive or even libelous speech.

New Directions for Adult and Continuing Education • DOI: 10.1002/ace

Communicate Honestly. Mentor and protégé must clearly and openly define their relationship and discuss the desired roles, goals, and outcomes of their association. Such clear communication may not be easy in the early stages of a relationship, when trust is less developed or information somewhat tentative. For example, in work with doctoral students this articulation may be a tentative timeline and the support desired from the mentor for completing key tasks. Mentors should take responsibility to communicate decisions they make regarding the relationship to their protégés.

Examine Power and Privilege. Because mentors have power and privileges that are not available to their protégés, they should carefully consider how their power can be helpful or hurtful in their work with protégés, and deliberatively use their power in positive actions for the good of their protégés and their work together. This may include ending the mentoring relationship and helping protégés find a mentor who is more able to help them toward their goals.

Conclusion

I am reminded of an old Buddhist saying: "No one is my friend, no one is my enemy, everyone is my teacher" (Buddhist Quotes and Sayings, 2005). Mentors are teachers, yet they are also students, learning from and with their protégés and others. As Freire (1997) contends, mentors should "transcend their merely instructive task . . . assume the ethical posture of a mentor who truly believes in the total autonomy, freedom, and development of those he or she mentors" (p. 324). These are lofty goals, yet attainable by mentors who consider and understand the ethics of mentoring as caring.

References

Buddhist Quotes and Sayings, 2005. Retrieved May 5, 2008, from http://buddhism. kalachakranet.org/resources/buddhist_quotes.html.
Caffarella, R. "Psychosocial Development of Women: Linkages to Teaching and Leadership in Adult Education." (Information Series 350). Columbus, Ohio: ERIC Clearinghouse on Adult, Career, and Vocational Education, 1993.
Daloz, L. *Effective Teaching and Mentoring: Realizing the Transformational Power of Adult Learning Experiences.* San Francisco: Jossey-Bass, 1986.
Darkenwald, G. G., and Valentine, T. "Factor Structure of Deterrents to Public Participation in Adult Education." *Adult Education Quarterly,* 1985, 35(4), 177–193.
Freire, P. (ed.). *Mentoring the Mentor: A Critical Dialogue with Paulo Freire.* New York: Peter Lang, 1997.
Hansman, C. A. "Formal Mentoring Programs." In A. Wilson and E. Hayes (eds.), *Handbook of Adult and Continuing Education.* San Francisco: Jossey-Bass, 2000.
Hansman, C. A. "Diversity and Power in Mentoring Relationships." In C. A. Hansman (ed.), *Critical Perspectives on Mentoring: Trends and Issues.* Columbus, Ohio: ERIC Clearinghouse on Adult, Career, and Vocational Education, Ohio State University, 2002a.
Hansman, C. A. "Mentoring and Continuing Professional Education." *Adult Learning,* 2002b, 12(1), 7–8.

man, C. A. "Power and Learning in Mentoring Relationships." In R. Cervero,
    Courtenay, and M. Hixson (eds.), *Global Perspectives: Volume III.* Athens, Ga.:
    University of Georgia, 2003.
Hansman, C. A. "Reluctant Mentors and Resistant Protégées." *Adult Learning,* 2005,
    14(1), 14–16.
Johnson-Bailey, J., and Cervero, R. "Cross-Cultural Mentoring as Context for Learning."
    In M. Alfred (ed.), *Learning and Sociocultural Contexts: Implications for Adults, Com-
    munity, and Workplace Education.* New Directions for Adult and Continuing Education,
    no. 96. San Francisco: Jossey-Bass, 2002.
Merriam, S., Caffarella, R., and Baumgartner, L. *Learning in Adulthood: A Comprehensive
    Guide* (3rd ed.). San Francisco: Jossey-Bass, 2007.
Noddings, N. "Caring: A Feminist Perspective." In K. Strike and P. L. Ternasky (eds.),
    Ethics for Professionals in Education: Perspectives for Preparation and Practice.
    New York: Teachers College Press, 1993.
Sissel, P. A., Hansman, C. A., and Kasworm, C. "The Politics of Neglect: Adult Learners
    in Higher Education." In C. A. Hansman and P. A. Sissel (eds.), *Understanding and
    Negotiating the Political Landscape of Adult Education.* New Directions for Adult
    and Continuing Education, no. 91. San Francisco: Jossey-Bass, 2002.

*CATHERINE A. HANSMAN is professor of adult learning and development (ALD)
at Cleveland State University.*

6

This chapter reflects on the ambiguity of ethical choices in adult education for democratic social change, especially in activities sponsored by traditional academic organizations.

Pursuit of Social Justice in Situations of Conflict

Tom Heaney

Stanley Fish, at the time a professor of both English and law at Duke University, narrated a story from the movie version of *How to Succeed in Business Without Really Trying* (Fish, 1994). Robert Morse, a young man fresh out of business school, is trying his wings in the corporate world and assigned to begin at the bottom—the mailroom. He soon discovers that his co-worker, an arrogant but oafish fellow, happens to be the nephew of the CEO. We learn that one of the two will be promoted to mailroom head and the person who will make the decision announces with great solemnity that he has been told to choose the new head on merit alone. The boss's nephew immediately responds, "That's not fair."

That's meant to provoke a laugh, of course, but the boss's nephew is perfectly serious! He has anticipated that, as the boss's nephew, he stood in a preferential position when promotions were handed out. He is outraged that the rules have been changed. The problem is not so much that "merit" is now the standard, but rather that, according to the prevalent understanding, being related to the CEO was a merit in its own right. Fish notes that, "In effect he is reacting just as the elder son in a hereditary monarchy might react were he to be told just before the king died that from now on we're going to do it differently and hold elections" (Fish, 1994, p. 3).

Concepts such as merit, fairness, and social justice cannot be understood univocally, without regard for social, economic, or political position. In fact, these words are generally positioned within a partisan agenda; they are the way contenders in a political struggle proclaim their vision of things

WILEY
InterScience®
DISCOVER SOMETHING GREAT

NEW DIRECTIONS FOR ADULT AND CONTINUING EDUCATION, no. 123, Fall 2009 © 2009 Wiley Periodicals, Inc.
Published online in Wiley InterScience (www.interscience.wiley.com) • DOI: 10.1002/ace.344

as normative. Representatives of a dominant paradigm will look at those who challenge them and say with full confidence, as did the boss's nephew, "It's not fair."

It is, of course, a practical strategy to appropriate the concept of merit and give it a meaning that serves my interests. However, I am not suggesting that terms such as *merit, fairness,* and *justice* should be abandoned. Rather, let me make a leap here to which I will return later and suggest that it is, in part, the role of an adult education practitioner to negotiate the use of such terms in multiple contexts. This is accomplished by peeling away layers of meaning and making explicit the agenda served by its use. The difficulty with pronouncements such as "it's not fair" or "it's not just" is that they are intended to silence opponents whose actions or positions threaten our own privilege—the status which culture, custom, and law have granted us.

"Fairness" and "justice" are, according to Gallie (1964), essentially contested concepts—concepts for which there are common understandings in the abstract, but disagreements over the application of these concepts to specific instances. Contested terms are often critical in ethical dilemmas—those times when we are faced with choices based on our interpretation of what is fair or what is just. The determination of what constitutes "social justice," what is fair or reasonable in human interactions, is always contextual and involves weighing the interests of self, others, and the social order. The concept of "order" is itself contested, representing social arrangements that benefit some more than others. It is in this situational quagmire that we struggle for definitions of justice.

As I think of my experiences as an adult educator committed to issues of social justice and fairness, many examples come to mind of instances in which my sense of what was just or what was fair differed significantly from the understanding of these concepts by others. Here are two examples of conflicting views of what is right and just in a situation.

Weighing Loyalties

Gilchrest Academy was an alternative high school for adults on Chicago's south side. Formerly a Catholic high school, Gilchrest became a satellite of the City Colleges of Chicago (CCC) in the midsixties, but the school maintained a high degree of independence. Students in this school, mostly African Americans, were dropouts and pushouts from public high schools. The curriculum was Freire-inspired and focused on social justice issues in the racially segregated and economically depressed Woodlawn community.

Administration in the CCC distrusted the school's activist stance in the turbulent decade of civil rights marches and the anti-Vietnam movement. Believing that public, academic institutions needed to maintain a neutral stance in the face of social controversy, some administrators tried to impose a less politicized curriculum on Gilchrest, without success. The growing distrust of the school was exacerbated by the fact that Gilchrest was more

New Directions for Adult and Continuing Education • DOI: 10.1002/ace

expensive to operate than other basic education programs in the community college system. Other programs minimized costs by employing part-time teachers who received no benefits and were not eligible to join the union. Gilchrest, however, because of its history as a Catholic institution, had a full-time, unionized faculty committed to transforming not just minds but conditions of life.

I was the liaison between the city colleges and Gilchrest and had a respectful, long-term relationship with its principal, teachers, and students. It was with a heavy heart that I learned that the chancellor of CCC, having failed several attempts to break the union, now wanted to close the program. He asked me to undertake a formal evaluation of the program with the clear, but unstated, expectation that my report would find the program deficient. He actually believed that the academic standards upheld by the school were low, based on the school's refusal to adopt the standard curriculum used in other more traditional programs.

From my prior experience with the school, I knew that my report was not likely to meet the chancellor's expectation. I began a monthlong onsite observation of classes and assemblies. I interviewed students, teachers, the principal, and members of the community board. I reviewed documents and, as I prepared my report, used focus groups of all the stakeholders—teachers, staff, students, community and union representatives—to shape and refine my analysis. In the end, the report became a self-study embraced by the entire Gilchrest community. Needless to say, the report was a disappointment to the chancellor, who promptly dismissed it as irrelevant to his intended purpose.

A month later, the chancellor held a meeting with the union representing the Gilchrest teachers. His intent was to announce the closing of the school. He handed them an evaluation study fabricated by a member of his staff, which challenged the academic integrity of the program and recommended closure. He was chagrined, however, when the union negotiator pulled out my original report and gave it to him. He did not realize that the method I had used in compiling the report included constant review of drafts by all members of the community, including union officials.

Gilchrest survived another year in the city colleges, as did I, but the gauntlet was down. Where there are conflicting values between a large institution, whose board is appointed by the mayor, and a neighborhood program, especially one committed to democratic social change, small victories are few and seldom long-lasting. Gilchrest was closed eventually—the result of reshuffling budget priorities.

One ethical dilemma faced by educators committed to social justice can be how to maintain employment without compromising the values of equity and justice. In defining what is just, we ask ourselves, Whom do we serve? When our obligations to students and the community conflict with the demands of our employers, what choices do we make? The complexity of our choices becomes even greater when we undertake work on behalf

New Directions for Adult and Continuing Education • DOI: 10.1002/ace

of oppressed communities—neighborhood programs in which a social change agenda can be too political or too radical for an academic institution to maintain an illusion of neutrality. There are communities whose interests are being overshadowed by developers in gentrifying areas. Do we serve the interests of low-income residents, or the interests of those seeking to "improve" the neighborhood? Do we support grassroots economic development, or colonization of a failed economy by outside interests?

These choices become more difficult when the institutions employing us are aligned with the power brokers in a community's struggle to regain control over their lives. As educators, we are seldom free agents. We are employed by and expected to represent the interests of educational institutions that are components of a larger social infrastructure and that are, in complex and frequently hidden ways, dominated by corporate and political interests.

Taking from Peter to Pay Paul

Basic education programs used to be "cash cows" in Illinois. The cost of basic education was low; classes in preparation for the GED, ESL, and literacy classes were reimbursed by the state at the same credit hour rate as were expensive on-campus courses in biology or science. That was about to change. The state legislature sought to vary reimbursement rates according to the actual cost of delivery. Courses requiring expensive equipment and supplies would generate far greater revenue from the state, whereas the reimbursement rate for basic education would drop by more than 70 percent.

Like Gilchrest Academy, Wentworth Education Center had learned to leverage a larger proportion of state reimbursement in support of its Freire-inspired program. I had worked with the team that created the center and served as liaison with the city colleges as well. Wentworth served more than two hundred Latinos and African Americans, many ex-offenders and former drug users. Its survival depended on funding at current levels. When the staff and students learned of the impending reduction, they decided to put their learning into action. They chartered two buses to take students and teachers to the state capitol, where they would demonstrate their opposition to the reduction of funding for their program and present their case directly to their elected representatives.

The morning they were to leave, they held a press conference in front of the school. The chancellor was at home shaving at the time, listening to a local news station when he heard the broadcast. What the teachers and students planning the demonstration did not know was that it was the chancellor who had engineered the planned reduction of funding in order to expand on-campus programming in other areas. The chancellor quickly cancelled his plans for the day and took a plane to the state capitol in Springfield. He arrived well before the buses and was on the steps of the capitol to greet his students and their teachers when they arrived.

New Directions for Adult and Continuing Education • DOI: 10.1002/ace

Press had been alerted and was well represented. This could have proven an embarrassing moment for the chancellor. However, he did what many leaders have learned to do; he observed the direction the people were moving, turned around and led them in the same direction. His actions were, of course, a source of confusion for the legislators whose help he had sought in moving the funding legislation forward. Despite the best efforts of the demonstrators and the false show of support by the chancellor, the legislation passed several weeks later and the Wentworth Center closed its doors within the year.

"Win-win" might be an effective strategy in negotiations, but decisions regarding prioritization of resources are unlikely to satisfy all. There will be winners and losers. Choices to divert funding to one sector of an educational enterprise impose a cost—at times a terminal cost—on another sector. One might believe that Wentworth Academy had been supported initially because of its success serving a marginalized population—something that would enhance the reputation of the community college system. More important, however, programs such as Wentworth had been a significant revenue source, netting hundreds of thousands of dollars annually in support of other academic programs. The fact that this program was abandoned when an alternative revenue source was identified gives lie to the presumption that the program's success was ever a factor in the earlier support enjoyed by the school.

There is also an underlying issue that affected both Gilchrest and Wentworth. Both programs placed social justice, equity, and democratic social change at the core of their curriculum. Students were learning to challenge the conditions of their depressed communities, to take an active role in decisions that affect their lives. In this they were mavericks within a fundamentally conservative and politically aligned institution. Ethical judgments about what is fair and just in relation to the self-interest of institutions beholden to markets and governments are inevitably at odds with the judgments of those oppressed by those same economic and political forces. Choices that benefit learners, especially those learners who are disadvantaged by systemic poverty, are frequently circumscribed by the organizational agenda of employers and institutions whose privilege is threatened by change.

Defining "Good Work"

As I reflect on my work with Gilchrest, Wentworth, and other similar grassroots educational organizations struggling to change the conditions of learners' lives, I have to ask how I came to determine that this was "good work." Goodness is, of course, along with justice and fairness, an essentially contested concept. For me, good work represents making the right choice among myriad alternative, and perhaps less controversial, options. My choice is guided by, Whom will I serve? This has been the foundational ethical question for me,

New Directions for Adult and Continuing Education • DOI: 10.1002/ace

which rose to clarity in the decade of the sixties, made explicit in the intensifying civil rights and anti-Vietnam War movements. The old labor organizing song, "Which Side Are You On?" crystallizes the ethical imperative I faced with endless televised images of violence against humanity in both the war abroad and the erosion of civil rights at home. Movements compel involvement; remaining a spectator is not an option. We are forced to take sides, but on what basis do we choose?

We each carry with us a set of values, culturally grounded, socially derived; these values become the basis of our choices. For some, these values are hegemonic, reflecting the normative influence of existing social arrangements (Gramsci, 1971). For others, resistance to persons and institutions that perpetuate oppressive conditions becomes a dominant value. It is this resistance that has guided my choice of sides in contentious situations. Rebelliousness and antiauthoritarianism, of course, do not guarantee that my choices have always been wise, or even ethical.

It is important to forge ethical decisions in the fire of critique, but it is also necessary to apply critique to our own pedagogy and allow our experiences of frustration and failure to become sites for learning. It is too easy to cast ourselves as heroes—a role totally inconsistent with a critical pedagogy (Horton and Freire, 1990) and strategically self-defeating. In acknowledging our failures, however well-intentioned, we move beyond instrumental knowledge about our best practices into the realm of emancipatory knowledge, revealing the assumptions, systems, and practices that result in blunders (Tassoni and Thelin, 2000). In a way unclear to me at the time, the stories of Gilchrest and Wentworth demonstrate blunders of the highest magnitude. Choices made resulting in short-term victories had long-term negative consequences for the communities served by those schools and also had a chilling effect on the future development of programs committed to social justice.

The essence of an ethical dilemma, of course, is that a choice can have both positive and negative consequences. How do I weigh these consequences? Or do I succumb to paralysis in the face of difficult choices? As an educator and as a citizen, I have tried to unveil and challenge my assumptions when faced with these choices—treat taken-for-granted solutions as problems to be solved democratically. Frequently frustrations encountered in life have been derived, in part, from the relentless pursuit of solutions to the wrong questions. So, we attempt to emphasize in educational work a critical approach to the analysis of day-to-day experience and practice—an approach that, to the extent we succeed, can reveal hidden assumptions and enable us to reassess the adult education enterprise in its social and historical context (Brookfield, 1995, 2004).

For many adult educators, action to change and sculpt social conditions is the point—the redeeming social purpose that inspired the adult education movement in the United States (Lindeman, 1961). In Lindeman's words, "Every social action group should at the same time be an adult education group, and I go even so far as to believe that all successful adult education groups sooner or later become social action groups" (cited in Brookfield, 1984, p. 192). As educators we hope to *inspire* learners to act on their own behalf, but also to *conspire* with others to effect social justice and change (Heaney, 1996).

Ethical choice and taking action, no matter how much forethought precedes them, always risk the making of mistakes, errors in judgment, or unanticipated consequences. Martin Luther's famous dictum *"pecca fortiter,"* translated as "sin bravely," emphasizes that the pursuit of justice is not without risk, but nonetheless it is a risk we must take (Faulkner, 1914).

Our choices have consequences, one of which is frequently that those choices put us in conflict with others.

Sources of Conflict

Ethical choices are made in the presence of power. That power can be overt with the demarcation clear, as when an employer directs our choice as a possible or presumed condition for continued employment. In the case of Gilchrest Academy, it was clear that my position as an administrator in the city college system would be irrevocably altered by the decision I made, even though my job was not directly threatened. My refusal to predetermine the results of an evaluation study and "spin" the evaluative report so that it would negatively affect the program placed me at a crossroad—my administrative colleagues and I taking divergent paths. However, my choice was not courageous. I was not in anyone's eyes a heroic figure facing a tank in Tiananmen Square. In truth, my choice was devious; I did not tell my supervisors either before or after the study was completed that the results of the study were in the hands of the Gilchrest union. I maintained my academic integrity, but I withheld information from the person who requested the report—information that he would have every right to assume I would provide. I did this knowing that the report would be ignored by the chancellor and, further, that having the report in the hands of the union would give Gilchrest an advantage in any showdown with the system negotiators.

There are instances, of course, where people are dismissed for doing what they believe to be right. These choices in the face of overt power are the most difficult ones to make. They are complex because, when the interests of the organization that employs us are diametrically opposed to the interests of those people whom we serve, then our own interests come into play—our interest in continued employment and in providing support for a family, for example. We are caught in the middle, where whatever we choose has harmful consequences. How we weigh these conflicting interests depends on the gravity of the harm inflicted by our choices. We are guided not by an absolute application of ethical imperatives, but by probabilities—achieving the greatest good for the greatest number.

New Directions for Adult and Continuing Education • DOI: 10.1002/ace

In such circumstances, power can be direct and in our face. More often, the exercise of power is subtler, operating in the background by normalizing an "order" in which a limited number of choices are appropriate or expected. Options are kept off the table, so that available choices are few. Bachrach and Baratz (1970) call this the "mobilization of bias," in which the focus is not on individual choices but rather on universal acquiescence to prescribed patterns of organizational behavior. Bureaucracy best exemplifies this manifestation of power in that it marshals our choices into narrow procedures and limited options. Federal and state policies, for example, regulate choices that affect what is possible in serving low-income adults by linking education with employment and adapting learners to marginal employment opportunities. What if it is clear that the authentic and self-proclaimed interest of these low-income adults is to develop the economic and political base of their communities?

Wentworth Center sought to politicize its students by encouraging action in and on behalf of community development, both politically and economically. As a consequence it fought for its survival in the state legislature and lost. Many programs serving populations with similar interests capitulate in the face of limited options. They follow the rules and mollify their academic patrons who underwrite a curriculum that at best leads to low-wage and unstable employment. These are choices made by educators with the best of intentions. Is it better to accept the limits imposed by public bureaucracies and academic sponsors? Or to risk everything by ignoring those limits and fight for one's own deeply held values? Which choice better serves learners? If our choices lead to the closure of a program, have our choices been just or fair?

I can legitimately question whether my choices have been the right ones, especially when I see programs committed to social justice—programs I have supported and encouraged to stay the course—destroyed in the inevitable conflict with their institutional sponsors. Ethical considerations precede our choices, but continue afterward as we reflect on actions taken and evaluate consequences.

The most insidious use of power is to keep even latent conflict from surfacing. This is what Stephen Lukes (1974) calls the "third dimension of power." Power here is a function of hegemonic forces and social arrangements that shape our wants and thereby limit our choices. Our values, and hence our ethical choices, are guided and shaped by what we uncritically read and what we see, by our day-to-day contact with colleagues, students, and employers. We construct ourselves subconsciously as citizens and educators over time and with a little help from our friends. As a result we find ourselves with colleagues and co-workers—all committed to ethical behavior but nonetheless working toward diametrically opposed social purposes. Only in the resulting conflict does the third dimension of power become visible. It is at this point we must ask, Who is benefiting from this conflict?

New Directions for Adult and Continuing Education • DOI: 10.1002/ace

Whose prospects and welfare are diminished? What interests are at play besides my own?

The Pursuit of Social Justice

In interrogating the conflicts and potential conflicts that follow our attempts to do good work like a shadow, we begin to understand the personal and societal values that our practice preserves, nourishes, impedes, or openly challenges—the instances in which "fairness" and "justice" have been defined to buttress our own privileges. We begin to analyze how our practice springs from, and connects to, our personal history and identity. We clarify key assumptions and organizing visions on which our practice is built and trace how these were autobiographically formed. What were the sources of these assumptions and visions? Experience, authority, theory, or something else? To what extent were our assumptions and visions culturally and politically sculpted? How were these assumptions and visions tested, altered, disbanded, or enlarged over time? It is in the painful honesty with which we address these questions that we move toward a more ethical stance and, blundering at times, advance the understanding and practice of what is fair and just.

Adult educators pursuing social justice frame their practice as a political activity, noting how issues of justice and fairness pervade and influence all that we do, and also recognizing how practice might promote injustice. We aim not merely to understand the relationship between practice and the world, but to change the relationship, to reinvent practice, to break down power inequities, and promote the well-being of others.

Our field has a rich tradition of this work, exemplified in the work of Myles Horton, Paulo Freire, John Ohliger, Father Jimmy Tompkins, Moses Cody, and many others who placed justice and fairness at the core of their practice. The tradition continues in the work of Phyllis Cunningham, Bud Hall, Larry Olds, Bob Hill, and many activist educators and popular educators, whose work on behalf of oppressed groups inspires and strengthens our own efforts to develop a sense of mission, to aspire to embrace "adult education as vocation" (Collins, 1991), and to determine and adhere to what is fair and what is just in our day-to-day encounters.

References

Bachrach, P., and Baratz, M. S. *Power and Poverty: Theory and Practice*. New York: Oxford University Press, 1970.

Brookfield, S. D. "The Contribution of Eduard Lindeman to the Development of Theory and Philosophy in Adult Education." *Adult Education Quarterly,* 1984, *34*(4), 185–196.

Brookfield, S. D. *Becoming a Critically Reflective Teacher.* San Francisco: Jossey-Bass, 1995.

Brookfield, S. D. *The Power of Critical Theory: Liberating Adult Learning and Teaching.* San Francisco: Jossey-Bass, 2004.

Collins, M. *Adult Education as Vocation: A Critical Role for the Adult Educator*. New York: Routledge, 1991.

Faulkner, J. A. "Pecca Fortiter." *American Journal of Theology*, 1914, *18*(4), 600–604.

Fish, S. *There's No Such Thing as Free Speech: And It's a Good Thing Too*. New York: Oxford University Press, 1994.

Gallie, W. B. "Essentially Contested Concepts." In *Philosophy and the Historical Understanding*. London: Chatto and Windus, 1964.

Gramsci, A. *Selections from the Prison Notebooks*. New York: International, 1971.

Heaney, T. *Adult Education for Social Change: From Center Stage to the Wings and Back Again*. Columbus: Ohio State University, ERIC Clearinghouse on Adult, Career, and Vocational Education, 1996.

Horton, M., and Freire, P. *We Make the Road by Walking: Conversations on Education and Social Change*. Philadelphia: Temple University Press, 1990.

Lindeman, E. *The Meaning of Adult Education*. Norman: Oklahoma Research Center for Continuing Professional and Higher Education, 1961.

Lukes, S. *Power: A Radical View*. New York: Macmillan, 1974.

Tassoni, J. P., and Thelin, W. *Blundering for a Change: Errors and Expectations in Critical Pedagogy*. Portsmouth, N.H.: Boynton/Cook, 2000.

TOM HEANEY *is the director of the adult education doctoral program at National-Louis University.*

New Directions for Adult and Continuing Education • DOI: 10.1002/ace

7

This chapter discusses three broad themes—reflection, power, and negotiation—that are evidenced in all of the practitioner chapters.

Reflecting on Reflecting on Practice

Arthur L. Wilson

Although it still remains orthodox to understand adult and continuing education as the procedural application of scientifically derived principles, its actual practice routinely requires judgments about what to do. Such choices are often murky as well as debatable in terms of intention and consequence. Even so, after much involvement in many aspects of adult and continuing education, and in particular the training of adult and continuing educators, I have come to the observation that adult educators often wish ardently (although not always consciously) for what one might call a level field of practice. On such a level field, intentions of all—student, teacher, administrator alike—would be clear and reasonable, there would be ample resources for supporting any and all effort, everyone would succeed, there would be no problems, and practice would be the flawless application of accurately defined procedures. Such a level professional field is, of course, utopian and never to be found in any profession, much less in adult and continuing education. Despite many decades of scholarly effort to produce a depiction of professional practice as level—that is, reasoned, scientifically validated, and morally certain—the real practice of adult and continuing education remains procedurally challenging, snared in questionable traditions, and morally ambiguous. Adult educators, whether practitioners or academics, simply do not have sure-fire theories, methods, or values that work all the time everywhere; nor are they likely to. Furthermore, despite nearly a century's worth of systematic investigation, there are still very few things we know for sure about adults, their learning, and our provision of it. Nor have our own understandings of what we are about remained even remotely

NEW DIRECTIONS FOR ADULT AND CONTINUING EDUCATION, no. 123, Fall 2009 © 2009 Wiley Periodicals, Inc.
Published online in Wiley InterScience (www.interscience.wiley.com) • DOI: 10.1002/ace.345

consistent; adult education in 2010 is a far different enterprise from adult education in 1920.

And that is just the background. As the chapters in this volume amply illustrate, the actual terrains of practice in ACE are extraordinarily diverse with various attendant ethical challenges. Donald Schön (1983) once contrasted the high and stable ground of academic inquiry, in which prescribed professional action is allegedly certain, with the low and swampy ground of actual professional practice in which action is always ambiguous and indeterminate. Richard Edwards (1997) has contrasted the "field" of academic adult education inquiry, in which "field" suggests clear boundaries to a well-ordered endeavor, with the "moorland" of practice, in which "moorland" animates the tractlessness and ambiguity of practice. The similarity of analogies is not coincidence; both portray aspects of a single phenomenon, the indeterminate nature of practice. Anyone familiar with traversing swamps or moorlands knows that the challenge of getting from one place to another is not simply a matter of following a well-trodden path, for there is none. Rather it requires the making of a path; indeed many possible paths may need to be brought into existence. Nor do ways that once worked always work again. So it is too in the swamps and on the moorlands of professional practice in which very little is ever certain because of the indeterminate nature of thought and action. On such terrains, not only are the technical demands challenging; so too are the moral claims about what we should be doing and whose interests we should be serving—which means we are always making choices about what is the best thing to do in any given situation. Such choices are rarely graced with certainty and exist routinely in competition with other possibilities. Because of that, adult and continuing education remains an endeavor of great ethical challenge—hence the merit of this volume.

I have been charged in this chapter to stand back a bit to view the effort of the volume. Typically, an academic approach would entail amassing and organizing the formal literature by which then to judge the effectiveness of the ethical decision making represented in the earlier chapters. Instead, I will use what might be referred to as an "immanent critique," with more emphasis on the immanent aspect and less on the critical one. *Immanent* refers to seeing from within, making sense of effort without imposing any external parameters (or as few as possible) in any event. Are there things we can learn from the efforts contained herein through concatenating their observations and questions? I think there is.

But first I offer a "preobservation," one that situates all the others though it is of a different category: the question of reflection. The practitioner chapters presume reflection on practice as both entry to and vehicle for a revealing and examining of ethical challenges inherent in practice. One thing that can be said about all the chapters is that each depends on the author's reflections. But I hasten to add that the chapters depend on rather variable notions of reflection; they do not represent a uniform construct, for it would be difficult to demonstrate that there is such uniformity. Let me illustrate.

The Swamp of My Earlier Practice

In the mid-1970s, I began working as an adult educator in a publicly funded adult basic education (ABE), high school equivalency diploma (GED), and English as a second language (ESL) adult learning center. In the conventions of the time, I was a "teacher" who was available to assist adults' learning, typically in an ad hoc, highly individualized, tutoring sort of way (we almost never used classes). Individualizing, in the theoretical and practical rhetoric of the time, was the preferred value or practice and was intended to mean that each student was "taught" according to her or his own particular needs and intentions. The reality was that too many adult educators, although genuinely espousing individualism, actually taught everyone the same way; they just did it one-on-one. The "good" teachers actually did customize instruction; they taught students individually, meaning they taught the prescribed curricula (for the GED test, for example) to various people depending on individual needs, abilities, and limitations. (How many ways can you teach how to divide fractions, correct subject-verb agreement, why the South lost the Civil War, or how to sound out iambic pentameter in a Shakespearean sonnet?) Over time I became one of those "good" teachers, able to transcend all kinds of boundaries. I developed multiple ways of teaching that accommodated and used culture, class, gender, race, and the myriad individual traits and histories each student presented. Further, as a matter of professional ethics, I cared greatly for students; I believed in them so that they believed in themselves. I personified the dominant humanist values inherent in that kind of adult education work, indeed as espoused more broadly across adult education efforts. Although I consciously wished to better my work (resulting in my first foray into adult education graduate study in the late 1970s), I also believed through conscious reflection that I was a good adult educator, doing the right sorts of things for adults who deserved that attention.

Yet as I reflected more and more on what I was doing, a doubt began to materialize and grow. Cancer like, it spread over time and poisoned my effort. Why, with so much good effort expended by others and me with similar values, abilities, and intentions, were we so spectacularly unsuccessful? We even had a term for it at the time: we creamed students. In the center in which I worked we might deal with a thousand students a year; maybe fifty would pass the GED test. Those fifty would have succeeded without our effort; we merely held their hand for a while. The rest would recycle repeatedly through the center and other social agencies in town; it was not unusual to see the same student a half a dozen times over several years, never really making educational progress except to continue to survive through clever and persistent use of available social support systems (such as adult learning centers). Because I was also involved with statewide staff development, I knew that other centers were experiencing similar results (and the adult literacy participation research has always confirmed this observation). We clearly were not helping the vast number of adult students in this setting, no matter how much training we had in learning styles, learning disabilities, individualized teaching methods, and so on. Or so I "reflected" at the time.

I do not mean to undermine the value of my insight then. It was genuinely perceptive, but not terribly useful. It did contribute to my moving on from ABE/GED/ESL. After eleven years of rather grueling work, I left to pursue other possibilities. There were many reasons for my leaving, but a chief one was this deep-seated sense of philosophical and ethical malaise that, despite what I thought were the right values, hopes, and efforts, I came to believe I was, fundamentally, doing a bad job. Indeed, subsequently I came to believe that while doing this work I was actually harming people with my efforts—but that realization came much later. The result is that I have never been able to return to the adult ABE/GED/ESL classroom since as a teacher.

What I have just described represents some orders of reflection. But as graduate students in my courses sometimes point out, this kind of reflection can be paralyzing, which in a way is what happened to me. Years after these experiences, however, I began to make new sense of them; I was less the protagonist but still greatly responsible. I lack the space here for a full account of what I have come to realize, but in brief it is this: that the large-scale failure of such effort was not entirely my own personal fault—that the failures of so many students was not entirely due to my inadequacies as a teacher. I have come to realize that such systems as I described above, despite their genuinely and expressly espoused values of care and hope, are actually fundamental to the social and educational reproduction of inequality in the United States. Designed to address the consequences of failing in American schooling, such systems actually perpetuate the continuing failure of those participating in them. I came to realize that the American schooling idea (to each her own achievement by her own bootstraps) had perversely pervaded the adult education ABE system in the United States. Through ideologies of "individualizing," we in effect were saying, "You who have already failed in the public school system will be given a second chance ostensibly to succeed but practically to fail again, because the obstacles to success are enormous." Individualizing, as a value of intention and a guide to practice, simply is inadequate to the task. In a blame-the-victim manner we systematically and systemically provided mechanisms for failure to continue to be reproduced, not simply for individuals but for whole classes of American citizens. Was I, am I responsible for such conditions? Yes, because my practice helped to perpetuate them. Was I, am I to blame? A less sure yes, but with growing awareness of selective structural conditions predicated on certain ideological frameworks that define opportunity for some and exclude others, then more so was I to blame. Was I aware, at that earlier time, of my embeddedness in a system of oppression, one in which I routinely but unreflectively and uncritically played out scripts that sustained the abilities of the system to determine who succeeded and who did not? At that time, no. But over time, first dimly and then more sharply, I had to come to accept my complicity in an allegedly well-intended but functionally oppressing schooling system. Many adult educators would vehemently disagree with such an indictment and deny responsibility for their role in it. But I counter that unless one is willing to forgo and break out of the dominating ideological stance in American education—that all merit is individually acquired and exercised regardless of race, gender, class, or any other social marker or conditions, and that success is solely defined by such effort—then my analysis will be vilified as excrement. In my view, it simply ain't so that individual effort is necessarily the major determinant of success.

I have just tried to illustrate different degrees of reflection. As noted earlier, there is a tendency to think of reflection as a unilateral construct when it actually may be many ideas. Reflection is often suggested as one of those traits that make humans human (although I question this, given that I think reflection is not limited to humans). Further, the idea of critically thinking about one's state in order to change practice is not new; it probably emanated most forcefully from Paulo Freire's *Pedagogy of the Oppressed* (1970), in the late 1960s and early 1970s in North American adult education. Schön in the 1980s developed the ideas of "reflecting on practice," although that work is preceded by Argyris and Schön's earlier organizational analysis of single- and double-loop learning (1974). The idea of critical reflection has gained great presence in North American academic adult education through the auspices and disciples of Jack Mezirow's work on transformational learning since the 1970s and 1980s (2000). At the risk of overstatement, critical reflection and transformational learning have supplanted the dominance of andragogy as a centering area of inquiry and ideology in at least U.S. adult education scholarship. Further, there has been a rather incoherent and unsustained effort to adopt the mantle of a sort of Schönian reflection on practice movement in North America that in my view has little softened the hardened arteries of scientific rationalism dominating the modern (technocratic) practice of adult education (with apologies to Malcolm Knowles). Even so, the ideas of reflection are not homogeneous and unilateral; there is not a single construct on which to depend, even though Mezirow and others have made efforts to parse out levels and hierarchies of reflection. I have tried to illustrate the potential for understanding reflection as a number of ethical possibilities, from awareness (have to start somewhere) to a critical personal insight (useful perhaps in individual improvement) to a more trenchant social accounting (the technical term is "reflexivity") that has far more explanatory power for assessing the practical and ethical consequences of professional action. The awareness and insight types appear to dominate our understanding of reflection currently; the social accounting type is where we should be heading if we are ever to improve the ethical practice of adult and continuing education. For example, Ronald Cervero and I have continued to develop one of the prime ethical stances of adult education in our work (Cervero and Wilson, 1994, 2006). In brief, we ask, Who benefits and who should benefit from our efforts as adult educators? To respond: we believe it is the ethical responsibility of adult educators to ensure that all who are involved in, have interest in, or stand to benefit from our efforts should be involved genuinely and substantively in the decision making about that effort. Many for a long time have promoted participation, but meeting such an ethical responsibility requires the practical structural analysis and insight I described earlier, by which I came to understand my complicity in systemic oppression. The ethical questions of "responsibility" cannot be effectively answered without the social accounting I described earlier, for awareness and personal insight typically do not make visible the structured conditions that produce systemic inequality, racism, sexisms, and other forms of oppression. (For those interested in reading more about this kind of reflexivity I would recommend Usher, Bryant, and Johnston, 1997; and Holland and Lave, 2001, for starters.)

I make two points here that relate to the practical ethics focus of this volume. First, we need to develop a better grasp of what we mean by reflection, what it means to do it, and why, because it actually can mean many things with numerous ethical consequences. Second, the sort of personalized reflection generally personified in this volume is a right step in producing a critique of practice. But in and of itself it is probably not sufficient to make radical shifts in how we understand our roles in the production and reproduction of systems that, in practice, may work against our expressed intentions. Thus we develop ethical issues because of a lack of congruence or integrity.

The Chapters

I will first return to the role of reflection in the production of the chapters as well as its role in changing practice. I have gone at it more generally above and more particularly below because I think it is the major thematic of the volume and one that is most problematic for both practice and study. Then I will turn to two other thematics that, until about the late 1980s, might have been noted tangentially through allusion (perhaps) but now seem to be more discrete centers of attention: power and negotiation.

Reflection. As already suggested, there are several forms of reflection represented in this volume, and given the range they have different consequences. Cathy Hansman's and Sue Folinsbee's efforts on mentoring and workplace literacy respectively each exhibit the sort of close, personal, critical scrutiny of their experience necessary for teasing out the ethical conundrums that often go unrecognized by the less insightful. Folinsbee notes how serious ethical questions are rarely analyzed in the formal literature. She describes using the "spiral model" as an articulated process that is similar to the reflection-on-practice that Schön (1983) describes as second nature in experienced practitioners. She learns from her practice to adjust her thinking toward realizing that formal prescriptions for institutional planning action (such as conducting needs assessments) may not always be expedient or necessary: "where one must adjust one's thinking about what principles mean in practice—remind us that even though principles remains steadfast, the practice we engage in needs to be flexible" (Chapter Three of this volume). Hansman takes a similar tack by reflecting on "my current role as a mentor and my past protégé role, knowing that because of the intense personal interactions between mentors and protégés, ethical issues can be sources of anxiety for both" (Chapter Five) in order to tease out practical responses to the ethical challenges of mentoring. Tom Heaney and Talmadge Guy in their own ways show indication of a more reflexive reflection. Guy examines his practice from the ethical challenges of "navigating" the influence and effect of "unmerited privilege" on educational interactions charged by racism and sexism. Heaney examines his and others' roles as he negotiates relations of power to sustain equitable treatment of Gilchrist Academy in the face of the City Colleges of Chicago's attempt to close the academy. Both demonstrate how "the socio-political, social, and cultural structuring of social existence is constituted in the daily practices and lived activities of subjects who both participate in it and produce cultural forms that mediate it" (Holland and Lave, 2001, p. 5). Further, they amply illustrate how what we typically take to be technical, procedural tasks in education—conducting a class, evaluating a program—are in fact deeply political activities with profound ethical responsibilities. Finally, in Anthony Weston's chapter there is evidence of my earlier point that we cannot presume unilateral meanings. His is probably the most reflexive chapter: "thinking about ethics is hard enough without having to think about thinking about ethics too" (Chapter One). Whereas it may not appear so, Weston's "meta-ethical" orientation is related to the reflexive orientation I described earlier as I came to understand more thoroughly how structural conditions forcibly scripted what I, colleagues, and learners could think and do. In fact, when the term is not being used as a synonym for reflection, "thinking about thinking" is often proposed as a form of reflexivity. What is different, though, is that the sort of analyzing of the situated scriptness of social practices in terms of their productive and reproductive capacities encourages a more precise political and ethical critique. I find the greater precision more conducive to imagining real change.

    Power. Power is a salient theme in all of the practitioner chapters. This is a very interesting development. It was not too long ago that formal discussions of power would have been impossible in the literature. Indeed, the formal literature eschewed such discussions as unseemly and unwarranted in order to promote scientific rationalism as a model of professional adult education practice (Cervero and Wilson, 1994, 2006; Wilson and Cervero, 1997). It is not that practitioners and scholars were unaware of the great effect of power on their work; they simply had no formal way of examining it. Through decades of prescriptions for professional practice, there are frequent allusions to the effects of power along with a demonstrated inability to comment directly (Cervero and Wilson, 2006). So it is promising to see power emerge so prominently. But I have to also comment that we have not made much progress in our understanding of power; as with reflection, there is a tendency to presume that we all know what power is, when actually power is many things.

I want to start this section by contradicting what I just wrote. Whereas most of the chapters take power as a central thematic, only Tom Heaney's actually theorizes the role of power in practice. To make ethical sense of his practice, Heaney explicitly draws on the famous "three faces of power debate" that raged from the 1950s to the mid-1970s, when power theorists from other disciplines moved beyond the behaviorist restrictions of the three-faces debate (Isaac, 1987; Nesbit and Wilson, 2005; Winter, 1996). Heaney describes forms of power as direct, "in your face"; power as the ability to "mobilize bias"; and power as a hegemonic force resulting from determinate social structures. These forms are very useful to know and distinguish because each requires its own practical responses. Talmadge Guy understands power as the functioning of unmerited privilege, in which he describes racism and discrimination as a function "of overt and covert privilege and white supremacy" (Chapter Four), another important understanding of power. Cathy Hansman implicitly adopts a realist understanding of power as capacity to act (Isaac, 1987) when she depicts a mentor's abilities "to remove oneself as a mentor . . . to challenge and inspire . . . to not communicate reasons for actions . . . to protect protégés" (Chapter Five). Sue Folinsbee understands the crucial role that power plays in any organizing of workplace education when she asks, "How do I work with those uneven workplace power relationships?" She answers by saying she has to "work to even out those power relations" (Chapter Three) by "balancing" the many interests at work. Although he does not discuss it directly, Anthony Weston's deliberative model of asking what each side is about, rather than which side is right, presumes the presence and effect of power. As with reflection, power is becoming ever more present in our efforts to understand and improve practice. But it is not a unilateral construct, and as the chapters show it has many facets and effects. There is a lot more about power than what shows up here; we cannot continue to presume that we all know what it is.

Negotiation. All the chapter authors discuss negotiation. At first glance, use of such a term, regardless of its many denotative and connotative uses, would seem appropriate in discussion about resolving dilemmas, choosing sides, and balancing interests. Indeed, it is appropriate here. What is remarkable, however, is that like power negotiation has not, until recently, had any place in our formal literature (Cervero and Wilson, 1994, 2006). Any human endeavor requiring social interaction will necessarily at times require negotiation because conflict, competition, and conflicting interests are always present in human interaction. But such negotiation of competing and conflicting interests has remained distant from the formal discussions in the field, which has constructed its identity as an applied science in which practice problems are solved by scientific knowledge (Wilson and Cervero, 1997). Understanding adult and continuing education as providing and using technical solutions to allegedly well-understood practice problems is only a small part of what educational work is about. Understanding the human-dimension aspects of practice, the "people work" (Forester, 1989), with the use of terms such as "negotiation," as these authors do, is as important as the production of "scientific" knowledge about adults and their education, if not more so.

Sue Folinsbee describes a situation I would take to be far more common than most of us are comfortable in recognizing. Caught among a zealous nonprofit board member, company management demanding accountability, and employees at risk of losing their jobs, Folinsbee somewhat ingenuously characterizes her deft intervention—clearly a very skillful negotiation—as being able to "convince" a manager of addressing the problem in a way that would facilitate its resolution. Tom Heaney calls for the adult education practitioner "to negotiate the use" in practice of contested terms such as "fairness," "merit," and "justice." Heaney is very clear that practitioners are "seldom free agents" and like other organizational workers are expected to understand and represent the interests of the organization. He portrays very complex negotiations between City Colleges of Chicago and Gilchrist in order to ask, How far can we go in furthering social justice causes and stay employed in the face of opposition from central forces? It seems to me that central to Anthony Weston's deliberative approach to figuring out what each side is about is also a process of negotiating. In her depiction of the powers that mentors have, Hansman portrays the complex negotiated personal human interactions required to sustain mentoring relationships, as when she realized that her sympathy for one of her students was actually disempowering the student. Talmadge Guy poignantly describes being "caught in an ethical bind in my teaching" as he struggles "to navigate [one of the many meanings of negotiate] a course of action that is simultaneously inclusive of multiple views and multicultural and antiracist, antisexist" (Chapter Four). To do so, he tries "to strike a balance between my commitment to an ethic of racial justice and inclusion . . . to strike a balance between my own positionality as an African American male and my privilege, authority, and power as a male professor" (Chapter Four). As with reflection and power, there is a lot going on in these chapters and thus a lot more to learn in order to improve this crucial activity of professional practice.

Final Comments

I have tried to transgress the chapters at some middling altitude to seek some broader thematics. To this end, my observations about reflection, power, and negotiation do transcend individual efforts, with reflection being the more prominent for my purposes and interests here. Without reflection of whatever sort, we diminish the likelihood of improving professional adult education practice. Without reflection there is little wherewithal to assess the ethical choices we make in the moorland and swamps of actual practice. Even so, there is still indeed much work to be imagined and enplotted in coming to better understand the roles of reflection, negotiation, and power. Without explicit direction or intended effect, these three major dimensions of our practice emerge in the chapters as prominent and insightful about what makes good practice. They help us understand the ethical challenges that we face more routinely than we may be willing to acknowledge.

More good news, to me anyway, is the sort of organic emergence of these themes (I realize I am an agent in such "emergence") as indicating something of a loosening of the stranglehold that the technical rational and instrumental portrayals and prescriptions of adult and continuing education practice have kept for so long on how we (are supposed to) understand our work. There is a "livedness" portrayed here that I easily recognize as real practice, and from which I can learn more about my work as an educator. These chapters are a vivid embodiment of what we adult educators have, for some time, claimed to be doing but, in my view, only very rarely actually achieved: reflecting on practice. These chapters give me hope: hope that maybe our profession can reinvent itself in a time of great constricting stress for the profession. We might actually do some of the good we say we are going to do.

References

Argyris, C., and Schön, D. A. *Theory in Practice: Increasing Professional Effectiveness.* San Francisco: Jossey-Bass, 1974.

Cervero, R., and Wilson, A. *Planning Responsibly for Adult Education: A Guide to Negotiating Power and Interests.* San Francisco: Jossey-Bass, 1994.

Cervero, R., and Wilson, A. *Working the Planning Table: Negotiating Democratically for Adult, Continuing and Workplace Education.* San Francisco: Jossey-Bass, 2006.

Edwards, R. *Changing Places? Flexibility, Lifelong Learning, and a Learning Society.* London: Routledge, 1997.

Forester, J. *Planning in the Face of Power.* Berkeley: University of California Press, 1989.

Freire, P. *Pedagogy of the Oppressed* (trans. M. Ramos). New York: Herder and Herder, 1970.

Holland, D., and Lave, J. (eds.). *History in Person.* Santa Fe, N.Mex.: School of American Research Press, 2001.

Isaac, J. *Power and Marxist Theory: A Realist View.* Ithaca, N.Y.: Cornell University Press, 1987.

Mezirow, J., & Associates. *Learning as Transformation: Critical Perspectives on a Theory in Progress.* San Francisco: Jossey-Bass, 2000.

Nesbit, T., and Wilson, A. "Power." In L. English (ed.), *International Encyclopedia of Adult Education*. Houndsmill, Basingstoke, Hampshire, UK: Palgrave-Macmillan, 2005.

Schön, D. *The Reflective Practitioner*. New York: Basic Books, 1983.

Usher, R., Bryant, I., and Johnston, R. *Adult Education and the Postmodern Challenge: Learning Beyond the Limits*. London: Routledge, 1997.

Wilson, A., and Cervero, R. "The Song Remains the Same: The Selective Tradition of Technical Rationality in Adult Education Program Planning." *International Journal of Lifelong Education*, 1997, *16*(2), 84–108.

Winter, S. "The 'Power' Thing." *Virginia Law Review*, 1996, *82*(5), 721–835.

ARTHUR L. WILSON *is a professor of adult education and chair of the Department of Education at Cornell University.*

8

In explaining their decision making and confronting their doubts, reflective and courageous practitioners show their critical and constructive thinking for handling the intellectual and interpersonal complexities of ethical analysis.

Doing "Good Work": Negotiating Possibilities in Ethical Challenges

Elizabeth J. Burge

After such elegant and thoughtful chapters, what may be useful as a closure to this volume? Bearing in mind the authors' reflections about sustaining an ethical mind-set, let us see which aspects may be particularly salient for today's complex and "untidy" contexts of practice.

Schön's famous comparison of the high and level ground away from the real action and the uncertain but challenging terrain of the swamp (1983, 1995) is invoked in the preceding chapter by Arthur Wilson: "Despite many decades of scholarly effort to produce a depiction of professional practice as level—that is, reasoned, scientifically validated, and morally certain—the real practice of adult and continuing education remains procedurally challenging, snared in questionable traditions, and morally ambiguous."

Talmadge Guy is equally frank about how his swamps of practice defy easy traverse: "The ethical principles of pluralism, inclusion, fairness, and justice turn out to be ideals to which we strive . . . not determinate paths we follow." Given such challenges, it is best to review how we might consider even the approach to ethical analysis.

Here Anthony Weston's inspiring arguments help. He proposes a "meta-ethical reorientation," new ways to think about how we conceptualize ethical analyses and decision making. He thinks past the usual choices offered between philosophical approaches and created by the oppositional positioning of components that surround an ethical issue. He challenges me to assess my own meta-ethical assumptions. Is my thinking always fixed into a dilemma-framing mode of analysis, or wedded to one set of theories?

NEW DIRECTIONS FOR ADULT AND CONTINUING EDUCATION, no. 123, Fall 2009 © 2009 Wiley Periodicals, Inc.
Published online in Wiley InterScience (www.interscience.wiley.com) • DOI: 10.1002/ace.346

(Not anymore!) He challenges me to "stay attentively and resolutely involved"—for example, to not regard an ethical situation as having static elements but as one with ongoing and changing dynamics. Avoid reductionist analyses, interrogate any context thoroughly as an ongoing dynamic with complicating factors in play, and examine the opportunity costs of any decision. The key to such thinking is my willingness to live with a compromise decision and get away from the strictures inherent in judging presumed right versus wrong options. Instead, look for where rightness may exist in the whole scenario: "begin to ask what *each* side is right *about*." In short, and in terms of his appreciation of the ethical deliberations of Sue Folinsbee, Talmadge Guy, Catherine Hansman, and Thomas Sork, sustain my focus on deep engagement in the issues of my practice and understand "exactly what is at stake." A balance is often the best outcome.

Arthur Wilson's meta-reflection on the Weston chapter and the narrative chapters refers to Schön's "reflective practitioner" (1983) stance and suggests how I might reach into my own experience. For example, I might usefully consider the difficulties of decision making inside the contested and competing landscapes I inhabit. Wilson outlines the challenge here: "We are always making choices about what is the best thing to do in any given situation. Such choices are rarely graced with certainty and exist routinely in competition with other possibilities. Because of that, adult and continuing education remains an endeavor of great ethical challenge." His reflective analysis of the four narrative chapters and Anthony Weston's chapter led him to three themes: reflection, negotiation, and power. All are multifaceted concepts, often covert in their operations and requiring serious engagement. As Talmadge Guy reminds me about that third theme, "Power yields nothing except with a struggle." Catherine Hansman illuminates some issues from her own values and experience. She refers to four loci of power in mentoring relationships, and how their effects and implementation led her to a stronger conviction to "deliberatively" "consider how [the mentor's] power can be helpful or hurtful . . . with protégés." At the very minimum, "do no harm." It all looks so obvious in print, doesn't it? But not easy in the heat of the action when one's capacity for detecting hegemonic discourse may be diverted. Tom Heaney's lesson here bears repeating:

In interrogating the conflicts and potential conflicts that follow our attempts to do good work like a shadow, we begin to understand the personal and societal values that our practice preserves, nourishes, impedes, or openly challenges—the instances in which "fairness" and "justice" have been defined to buttress our own privileges.

Six Other Lessons

First, know your own ethical principles and which ones would send you (metaphorically) to the barricades in defense. Sue Folinsbee, for example, outlines five principles, of which inclusion and privacy are key. Workers deserve full confidentiality, even against management pressures: "I do not see *any* circumstances that would warrant making such risk-inducing personalized results available to management, or the union for that matter." Catherine Hansman values especially the ethic of care; Tom Heaney, fairness and social justice; and Talmadge Guy, equitable participation and critical dialogue.

Second, develop a personalized model to analyze your experience and ethical decision making, during and after the action. Sue Folinsbee's Spiral Model helps her reflect on workers' and trusted colleagues' experiences, and then analyzes any developing patterns for generating new knowledge for the next sequence of activity. Her intuition plays a major signaling role. Tom Sork acknowledges the Brockett and Hiemstra "ethical decision making" model and responds to Nash's framework, each designed to help practitioners interrogate their own driving values as well as the surface ethical issue, its influencing context, and the ranges of possible other issues even before resolutions are explored.

Third, use a primary question to reclaim your guiding value and steer your analysis of conflicting constituencies and their needs. The stated focus is on the client, the recipient(s) who ought to gain most from our activities: "Who is the client?" (Folinsbee). "Whose interests do we serve? Do we serve the interests of low-income residents, or the interests of [developers] seeking to 'improve' the neighborhood? Do we support grassroots economic development, or colonization of a failed economy by outside interests?" (Tom Heaney).

Fourth, critical thinking is the *raison d'être* of an ethically minded practitioner. Otherwise opportunities for close examination—indeed, excavation—of unchallenged assumptions, antinomies, and so on will be lost. Arthur Wilson, for example, argues for societal structural-level analyses in order to identify sites of ethical dissonance. He advises us to "make radical shifts in how we understand our roles in the production and reproduction of systems that, in practice, may work against our expressed intentions. Thus we develop ethical issues because of a lack of congruence or integrity."

Fifth, understand how to identify and balance competing interests. They may act as a minefield until all the layered factors are unearthed and assessed for potential impact. When agency or governmental agendas act negatively on the adult educator, the related institution, and the intended recipients of that institution's services, how are ethical decisions made to reduce anticipated negative effects on those recipients? Catherine Hansman shows one example when she explains how she challenged some of her own colleagues' denigrations ("trash talk") of her students in order to protect her protégés; but she knows that such defenses create follow-on risks, for example, her own professional exclusion by those colleagues, or worse. Another example is her need to plan a balanced response between giving frank feedback to students and not damaging their overall self-esteem. Sue refers to a quartet of over and covert competing interests in a workplace: "We may have to work with all the interests held by the levels of management and workers, along with funders' and educators' own institutional interests." One final example is a common one: the educator is forced to abandon adequate needs assessments in order to run enough predesigned programs to meet the revenue targets of her or his employer.

Sixth, understand where you and your values fit in the larger institutional and societal dynamics surrounding an ethical issue. Where do your obligations ultimately lie? "As educators, we are seldom free agents. We are employed by and expected to represent the interests of educational institutions that are components of a larger social infrastructure and that are, in complex and frequently hidden ways, dominated by corporate and political interests" (Heaney). When challenging dominant social interaction patterns and attitudes, as Guy does regarding whiteness, stay alert to the possibility of reverse dynamics and counterclaims of unethical behavior from those who refuse to change their perspective.

Ultimately, there is no room for heroic posturing or going down in the flames of unrealistic promises. Allied to such acceptance is the need to avoid "the relentless pursuit of solutions to the wrong questions" (Heaney). But there is much room for clear-eyed, even courageous, self-analysis, especially after things have gone wrong or when the success of a project was all too fleeting. Only then may an ethical practitioner get past recalling procedural skills or descriptions of what went wrong and instead apply the more challenging skills of critical self- and decision-making analyses. As Heaney learned, social justice projects are not designed easily, nor the social injustice itself ameliorated quickly. Responding to them involves challenging covert power structures that may in turn create significant long-term dangers for the adult educator and her or his participants.

To summarize, relentlessly detailed critical thinking, principled flexibility, and calm negotiation apply. Above all, take the broad view and seek a balance between competing dynamics. Negotiate for resolutions, and don't abdicate value-driven stances.

Questions for an Ending

These questions are framed by Tom Sork's assessment of some current, powerful intersecting dynamics in our field: "What does seem clear is that the moral dimensions of practice will become even more complex as concerns about the environment, inclusion, respect, and diversity interact with changes in technology, the economy, and emerging institutional forms in adult and continuing education."

So where next? Do we need another research project to illuminate current ethical concerns of adult educators, this time using several countries for data gathering? Count me in. Might we investigate practitioner perceptions of how moral ambiguity plays out in the trenches? Count me in. Is there any point in returning to code-of-conduct discussions? Might we revisit our trenches for deeper reflexivity? How to help those with lesser swamp experience interrogate and manage competing needs, seeming clashes of values, and covert power differentials? How might we engage with professionals in related fields, to "invite [ourselves] into a broader field of possibility"? (Weston chapter)

Finally, Arthur Wilson's reflections reveal some confidence in his expectations: "These chapters give me hope: hope that maybe our profession can reinvent itself in a time of great constricting stress for the profession. We might actually do some of the good we say we are going to do." Feel encouraged.

References

Schön, D. A. "Knowing in Action: The New Scholarship Requires a New Epistemology." *Change,* 1995, 27(6), 27–34.
Schön, D. A. *The Reflective Practitioner.* London: Temple Smith, 1983.

ELIZABETH J. BURGE is a professor in adult education at the University of New Brunswick in Atlantic Canada and a community social activist.

INDEX

93

Defoe, T., 37, 40
Dewey, J., 12, 14, 49
Dilemma-ism, 10–12
Duke University, 65

Edwards, R., 76
Elias, J. L., 19
English as a second language (ESL), 77, 78
English temperament, 15
Equitable participation, 89
ESL. *See* English as a second language (ESL)
"Ethical bind," 17
Ethical challenges, negotiating possibilities in, 87–91
Ethical decision-making (EDM) model, 26
Ethical dilemmas, 10–12
Ethical issues, 48–50; in mentoring adults in higher education, 53–62
Ethical Practices Analysis (Sork), 26
Ethical theories, 14–15
Ethics: codes of, 20–25; importance of, 20; in practice of adult education, 15–18
Ethics, applied. *See* Applied ethics
Euro-Western ethical perspective, 28

Fairness, 66, 69, 89
Faulkner, J. A., r6
Felch, W. C., 19
Financial institutions: and curriculum, 37; and educational institutional expectations *versus* real workplace needs, 38; and mandatory participation, 37; and overpromising benefits, 38; and power relationships, 36–37; and serving interests, 36; understandings of literacy in, 37; and workplace literacy, 35–38
Fish, S., 65
Folinsbee, S., 1, 4, 16, 34–37, 40, 80–83, 88, 89
Forester, J., 83
Frank, Fiona, 36
Freedman, E. B., 48
Freeman, M. K., 21
Freire, P., 23, 62, 66, 68, 70, 73, 79

Galbraith, M. W., 19
Gallie, W. B., 66
Garcia-Zamor, J.-C., 21
GED. *See* High school equivalency diploma (GED)

Georgia, 46
Germanic Protestantism, 15
Gilchrest Academy (Chicago), 17, 66–71, 81
Gilligan, C., 11
"Good work," 69–71
Goodness, concept of, 69
Gordon, J. C., 26
Gordon, W., 22, 23
Gouinlock, J., 12
Gramsci, A., 70
Griffith, W. S., 21
Guglielmino, L. M., 19
Guidelines for Development and Implementing a Code of Ethics for Adult Education (Coalition of Lifelong Learning Organizations), 22
Guy, T., 1, 4, 17–18, 43, 81, 83, 87–90

Hall, B., 73
Hansman, C., 1, 4, 16, 53, 54, 57, 60, 80–83, 88, 89
Hatcher, T., 21
Heaney, T., 1, 4, 16, 17, 65, 71, 73, 81–83, 89, 90
Heinz Dilemma, 10–12, 14
Henriques, D. B., 20
Hiemstra, R., 1, 2, 19, 26, 89
High school equivalency diploma (GED), 77, 78
Hill, B., 73
Hippocratic Oath, 61
Holland, D., 80, 81
Holt, M. E., 19
Hooks, b., 48
Horton, M., 23, 70, 73
How to Succeed in Business Without Really Trying (movie), 65
Hunter, J., 37, 40

Ianinska, S., 21
Illinois, 68
"Immanent critique," 76
Inclusion, 88
Indiana, 21
Individualizing, theories of, 78
Industry Standards for Classes with Potential Commercial Content (Learning Resources Network), 20
Interests, serving, 36
Issac, J., 82

Jackson, N., 37, 40
James, C., 34

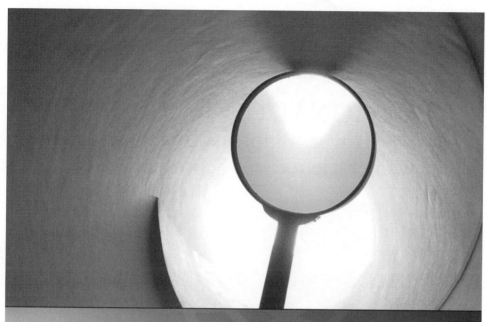

Why Wait to Make Great Discoveries

When you can make them in an instant with
Wiley InterScience® Pay-Per-View and ArticleSelect™

Now you can have instant, full-text access to an extensive collection of journal articles or book chapters available on Wiley InterScience. With Pay-Per-View and ArticleSelect™, there's no limit to what you can discover...

ArticleSelect™ is a token-based service, providing access to full-text content from non-subscribed journals to existing institutional customers (EAL and BAL)

Pay-per-view is available to any user, regardless of whether they hold a subscription with Wiley InterScience.

Benefits:

• Access online full-text content from journals and books that are outside your current library holdings
• Use it at home, on the road, from anywhere at any time
• Build an archive of articles and chapters targeted for your unique research needs
• Take advantage of our free profiled alerting service the perfect companion to help you find specific articles in your field as soon as they're published
• Get what you need instantly no waiting for document delivery
• Fast, easy, and secure online credit card processing for pay-per-view downloads
• Special, cost-savings for EAL customers: whenever a customer spends tokens on a title equaling 115% of its subscription price, the customer is auto-subscribed for the year
• Access is instant and available for 24 hours

WILEY
InterScience®
DISCOVER SOMETHING GREAT

www.interscience.wiley.com

Photography: Paweł Rosolek

47760b

YOUR free ISSUE OF
NATIONAL CIVIC REVIEW
is now available online. Go to
www.interscience.wiley.com/journal/NCR

In this Issue:

- Public Employees as Partners in Performance: Lessons From the Field *by Brooke A. Myhre*
- Starting Performance Measurement From Outside Government in Worcester *by Roberta Schaefer*
- Current Approaches to Citizen Involvement in Performance Measurement and Questions They Raise *by Anne Spray Kinney*
- Bridging the Divide Between Community Indicators and Government Performance Measurement *by Ted Greenwood*

WILEY
Publishers Since 1807